SALT PORK AND POOR
BREAD AND WHISKEY

Governor John Brown Francis (1791-1864). Photograph ca. 1860.

SALT PORK AND POOR BREAD AND WHISKEY

The Adirondack Diaries of John Brown Francis

Edited by

Henry A. L. Brown

HERITAGE BOOKS
2013

HERITAGE BOOKS

AN IMPRINT OF HERITAGE BOOKS, INC.

Books, CDs, and more—Worldwide

For our listing of thousands of titles see our website
at
www.HeritageBooks.com

Published 2013 by
HERITAGE BOOKS, INC.
Publishing Division
100 Railroad Ave. #104
Westminster, Maryland 21157

International Standard Book Numbers
Paperbound: 978-0-7884-0732-1
Clothbound: 978-0-7884-6904-6

To my wife
Ann Eckert Brown

CONTENTS

ILLUSTRATIONS

following page 62

FOREWORD

In 1988 the Rhode Island Historical Society published *John Brown's Tract: Lost Adirondack Empire* by Henry A.L. Brown and Richard J. Walton. The work was seen as one of several projects to mark the 200th anniversary of the John Brown House in Providence. It was also seen as an important piece of scholarship that supplied a missing chapter in the well-known story of a leading early American entrepreneur and his family. While it is customary to measure historical figures of business and industry by their positive accomplishments, it is also sometimes equally instructive to analyze their failures.

John Brown's Tract was, in its time, a huge expanse of Adirondack wilderness. To be sure, there were timber and mineral resources on the tract of a scale to match the grand vision of John Brown. Equally grand, however, were the climatic and environmental obstacles preventing that vision from being fulfilled. While some may argue that John Brown's death in 1803 hampered the development of the tract by removing a dynamic, persistent force so necessary for wresting a fortune out of a stubborn fastness, yet it is hard to imagine that even the "cleverest boy in Providence Town," as he once described himself, could have produced a much more favorable result than the efforts of his luckless son-in-law, Carl Friederich (Charles Frederick) Herreshoff, or his beloved grandson, John Brown Francis.

Lost Adirondack Empire amply illustrates the dumbfounding and numbing events that stymied all efforts to unlock this storehouse of wilderness wealth. Thus it was with interest, but also with some foreknowledge that I picked up Henry Brown's edited diaries of John Brown Francis's visits to the tract in 1816, 1817, and 1818. John Brown Francis had almost as distinguished a career as his accomplished grandfather. He served a string of terms as Governor of Rhode Island in the 1830's and went on to the United States Senate. He was a lifelong businessman and tried many efforts—most of them successful—at scientific agriculture. Although his trips to the Adirondacks occurred when he was a young man in his twenties, he was a young man with an already well-formed view of the world and human nature. This sophistication makes his diaries, particularly the first one, very interesting to read.

The diaries are like the core of a soil sample drilled into the mass of original manuscript material that formed the foundation of the documentation for the *John Brown's Tract* book by Henry Brown and Richard Walton. Although the diaries comprise only a fraction of the total mass of the documentation, much like a good core sample, almost all the key elements of the story are found in the diary in abbreviated form. For example, the constant adverse weather conditions on the tract are stated matter-of-factly by the simple diary entries reporting frosty mornings in July and August.

There are references to the crushing reverses caused by collapsing improvements, like the recently built bridges that were carried away by recurring floods. There were other improvements that fell into almost immediate decay. These dire developments underline the heroic struggles required to cut roads into the wilderness necessary to move the iron products out to the markets in the thoroughfare towns of Utica and Albany. Reports of failed crops and depletion of animal stocks suggest the difficulties in converting the forest to agricultural pursuits. Although the diaries cover only a few years, they are prescient forecasts of decades of failed attempts to transform the forest into a fertile hinterland.

A more positive note in the diaries is found in the series of personality vignettes sketched by John Brown Francis from his encounters with people en route to the tract and on the tract itself. From tavern keepers and toll collectors to farmers' daughters and land barons, little of the human condition escapes the eye of the youthful annalist. While most of our insights into the population of the early American frontier stem from the observations of foreign travelers like DeTocqueville, Mrs. Trollope and Dickens, here, for historians of the early republic, is a whole fresh catalogue by an American reporter.

Salt Pork and Poor Bread and Whiskey and its larger sibling, *John Brown's Tract,* serve to remind historians who write about the "Age of Boundlessness" that the years after the War of 1812 were not all success stories. Some writers have inferred that once the British and Indian threats to the Old Northwest were removed by the Peace of Christmas Eve in 1814, the settlement of the Appalachians and the Mississippi Valley was one long series of inevitable triumphs. The bleak results of efforts in the Adirondacks during this period offer a different proof that the march of progress into these frontier hinterlands was hardly a walk in the park.

ALBERT T. KLYBERG
Director
Rhode Island Historical Society

ACKNOWLEDGMENTS

I am grateful to all the librarians, historians, town clerks and staff of the following institutions who assisted my research:

Adirondack Book Club, Saranac Lake, N.Y.; The Adirondack Museum, Blue Mountain Lake, N.Y.; Amsterdam (N.Y.) Free Library; Berkshire Athenaeum, Pittsfield, Mass.; Brookfield (Mass.) Town Hall; John Carter Brown Library, Brown University; Clapp Memorial Library, Belchertown, Mass.; Connecticut Historical Society, Hartford; Constable Hall Association, Inc., Constableville, N.Y.; Grey Otis House, Boston; Little Falls (N.Y.) Public Library; Merrick Public Library, Brookfield, Mass.; New England Geneal-ogical Society, Boston; The New-York Historical Society, Coopers-town; New York Public Library; New York State Education Department Cultural Education Center, Albany; New York State Historical Association, Cooperstown; New York State Library, Albany; Pittsfield (Mass.) Public Library; Plattsfield (N.Y.) Public Library; Rhode Island Historical Preservation and Heritage Commission, Providence; Rhode Island Historical Society, Provi-dence; Schenectady County (N.Y.) Historical Society; Society for the Preservation of New England Antiquities, Boston; Sturbridge Village (Mass.) Library; Union College Library, Schenectady, N.Y.

For their help in recommending or providing background material, I am especially grateful to my mother, Susanne R. Lewis Brown (who also helped me decipher the handwriting in the diaries), my brother, Francis Hail Brown, and my cousin, Eleanor Fair Brown; and to many others, including Richard Sanders Allen; Elizabeth B. Bilobrowka; Richard A. Cohen; Edward Comstock, Jr.; James Corso and Paul Meker of the New York State Library; Rose Marie Fowler; Nathanael Greene Herreshoff; Albert Klyberg, Director of the Rhode Island Historical Society; Joyce Knibb, town historian, Burrillville, Rhode Island; Helen Lister; Averill Maher, treasurer of the Burrillville Historical and Preservation Society; Robert W. Merriam; Edith Pilcher; Emily Piper; and Rita Warman, librarian at the Merrick Public Library.

I am indebted to Janet M. Phillips for her work in copyediting, typesetting, and laying out the manuscript in book form, as well as her encouragement throughout the publishing process. Joan Lane Gordon undertook the exacting task of transcribing and typing the first draft from John Brown Francis's original diaries, and Ted Comstock provided additional editorial input. Finally, I want to express my heartfelt gratitude to my wife, Ann Eckert Brown, for her patience, practical help and moral support in the preparation of the journals.

HENRY A.L. BROWN

EDITORIAL METHOD

Because a diary's impact lies in its sense of immediacy and intimacy, virtually all original spelling and punctuation have been retained, without resorting to [sic] and other distractions. Only where a word or reference is unclear are clarifications or a question mark inserted in brackets. For the same reason, where the diarist underlined words for emphasis, the underlining is reproduced rather than converted to italics.

INTRODUCTION

I grew up in the 1930s and '40s on the ancestral farm known as Spring Green, overlooking Occupastuxet Cove in Warwick, Rhode Island. The farm's recorded history dates back to 1642, when Deputy Governor John Greene obtained title to it from the Narragansett Indian chief Miantonomo. It was purchased from the Greenes (and named Spring Green) in 1783 by the merchant John Brown, one of the founders of the Brown dynasty in Providence. Brown's grandson, John Brown Francis (1791-1864), spent his own childhood here, and inherited the farm on the death of his mother, Abby Brown Francis, in 1821.

John Brown Francis went on to distinguish himself as one of Rhode Island's leading citizens. Trained in the law, he was elected to the Rhode Island legislature in 1818, then ran for governor in 1832, serving five successive one-year terms. In 1844 he went to Washington to serve out the unexpired term of Senator William Sprague, who had resigned after the murder of his brother Amasa. He also served as Chancellor of Brown University (his alma mater) from 1851 to 1854.

Francis married twice: first in 1822 to his cousin Anne Brown (only daughter of Nicholas Brown, Jr.), who bore him two daughters and a son. Anne died in 1828, and only one child, Anne, survived to adulthood. In 1832 Francis married his cousin Elizabeth Francis. They had four children, two of whom—Elizabeth and Sally—lived to adulthood. These maiden sisters adopted their five-year-old cousin Alice, daughter of Charles W. and Eulalie McGuire Francis, after Eulalie died young, leaving six children. Little Alice thus became John Brown Francis's adopted granddaughter, and the eventual heir to Spring Green Farm. Alice Francis (Mrs. Frank Hail Brown) was my grandmother.

John Brown Francis's name and title are still associated with this part of Warwick. A portion of Spring Green Farm's 640 acres was subdivided into house lots in the 1930s by my grandfather, father, and uncle, who named the new development Governor Francis Farms. They also donated to the city of Warwick a parcel of land for the erection of the John Brown Francis elementary school, dedicated in 1952. The Governor Francis shopping center nearby (the city's first) was built after World War II.

Relics of an earlier era were woven into the fabric of my childhood. When I was a boy, Spring Green Farm was little changed from the nineteenth century: we cut ice and chopped wood in the winter, hayed in the summer using horse-drawn equipment, and milked a herd of dairy cows. The "grapery," a greenhouse built by John Brown Francis, gave shelter from the icy blasts of January and February. Century-old orchards of apple and pear planted by the governor still bore fruit, until blown down in the great hurricane of September 1938.

On the third floor of the Greene family's original house (ca. 1690), my grandfather's bedroom, with its ceiling-to-floor double doors, overlooked the broad expanse of the west meadows. This, I was told, was John Brown Francis's favorite view when it was his own bedroom. Then there was John Brown's elegant chariot, circa 1782, stored in an outbuilding. (It is now at the John Brown House museum in Providence.) My grandfather, Frank Hail Brown, delighted in showing off this grand old vehicle to visitors.

Family letters indicate that young John Brown Francis accompanied his grandfather on a trip to Utica, New York in this very carriage, on business related to the attempted settlement of John Brown's vast land holdings in the Adirondacks. The 210,000-acre "Brown's Tract" was purchased in 1797-8, in an era of rampant land speculation, by John Brown Francis's father, who was John Brown's son-in-law and business partner. John Brown planned to leave a "handsome fortune" to his grandson, and he intended the Adirondack land to make up a good part of that fortune.

In the 1950s I inherited a Sheraton linen chest belonging to the Francis family. It contained a small locked wooden box which, when opened, revealed a number of John Brown Francis's letters to his children, written during his years in the Senate (1844-45). Two small notebooks also fell out—one leather bound, both very worn with use. They were the handwritten journals of Francis's travels to, from, and on the Brown Tract in 1816 (Volume I), 1817 and 1818 (Volume II), as he continued the family's struggle to settle the Adirondack wilderness and wring a profit from it.

The larger story of Brown's Tract has been told in a book I co-authored with Richard J. Walton, *John Brown's Tract: Lost Adirondack Empire* (published by the Rhode Island Historical Society, 1988). Francis's diaries tell his own side of this arduous and sometimes tragic saga, as well as giving us a keyhole view of the times, the turnpike- and canal-building era, tavern life, and the westward march of the American frontier. They are also a window into the mind of a well-read, intelligent and self-assured young man, keenly observant of everything and everyone around him, who often resorts to philosophical musings and recitations of Shakespeare to relieve the tedium and hardship of frontier life.

Francis, age 25, arrived on the Tract in 1816 after a two-week journey on horseback from Providence. He had recently graduated from the first law school in America, founded by Judge Tapping Reeves in Litchfield, Connecticut, and lost no time in promoting his own interests and those of his family. He submitted to the New York legislature in 1816 a proposal that "would be useful to the public & beneficial to the owners of land through which a road would pass northly from Boonville intersecting the road leading from Albany to the St. Lawrence." The legislation was duly enacted for the road, and John Brown Francis and two business partners were appointed commissioners to survey and lay out the route.

The role of mediator and adjudicator for the Brown family's interests in New York now lay with Francis, at least while he was on the Tract. He was thus able to shoulder some of the responsibilities borne by his 56-year-old uncle, Charles Frederick Herreshoff, whose own herculean efforts to develop the Tract while living there year-round—largely isolated from family and friends—eventually broke his spirit and drove him to suicide.

Francis, although an aristocrat by American standards and not lacking in self-regard, was hardly a pampered upperclass fop. He plunged into the task at hand and worked alongside his crew, exploring and surveying a remote wilderness in conditions that most of us in the twentieth century could scarcely imagine, much less withstand. His disdain for those who led a more cosseted life is evident in an offhand remark in the 1818 diary about his cousin Nicholas Brown's unexpected visit to the Tract: "He had no conception of the distance or state of the road or not a bribe would have got him here."

John Brown died in 1803 and by his will John Brown Francis eventually controlled over 102,000 acres of Adirondack land. Years later he referred sardonically to his "good fortune" in the value of township No. 7, of 23,180 acres (one of eight sections in all). Francis wrote, "This was a part only of a Moon shine inheritance giving me the appearance of wealth but in reality fastening poverty upon me."

In hindsight, the only surprising aspect of that realization is how long it took the Brown family to realize the folly of attempting to turn a high, rocky, densely forested wilderness into farmland. (Two centuries later, the Adirondack region is still largely undeveloped; much of it has been designated a wilderness preserve.) Perhaps the toughness and perseverance of New Englanders, who had already tamed a difficult land, made it harder for them to foresee or admit defeat in such an enterprise. Moreover, the efforts of DeWitt Clinton, who became New York State canal commissioner in 1810, seemed to open up great possibilities for the Tract.

After Clinton was elected governor in 1817, the New York legislature passed his bill to continue the "Grand and Western canal." This 360-mile navigable waterway, renamed the Erie Canal, linked the Hudson River with Lake Erie. A canal advocate rhapsodized that it "will promote agriculture, manufacture and commerce, mitigate the calamities of war ... and enhance the blessings of peace, consolidate the union, advance prosperity and elevate the character of the United States"—in the process increasing the value of land in New York, Ohio, and the midwestern territories. (The Brown and Francis families also owned raw land in Ohio). Report followed glowing report, speaking of the great riches to be generated by the canal. In fact, once opened in 1825, it allowed settlers to bypass the Adirondacks for the rich bottomlands and kinder climate of Ohio. But for a short time the value of Brown Tract land soared, and the family continued throwing good money after bad.

In the last analysis, though, their experience was not all on the debit side of the ledger. Whatever hardships and losses Francis endured as a result of his "Moon shine inheritance," the enterprise and grit that he shows in these journals served him well throughout his life and undoubtedly made him a better public servant.

Early writers on the history of John Brown's Tract "avowed it to be shrouded in almost impenetrable mystery" (according to Alfred L. Donaldson's authoritative *History of the Adirondacks*). It is a great pleasure to be able to shed additional light on that mystery, and on the life and career of one of Rhode Island's most prominent nineteenth-century citizens, with the publication of these journals.

HENRY A.L. BROWN
Spring Green Farm
April 1997

The Adirondack Diaries of John Brown Francis

Part I: 1816
Part II: 1817
Part III: 1818

6 August 1816

Left Providence on horseback the 6th of August 1816, a sultry day. Stopped at D. Angell in Smithfield[1] & again in Burrillville 14 miles. Enter Massa. in Uxbridge, then to Douglas. Thro' a corner of Sutton to Oxford & lodge at Campbell's,[2] 30 miles. The road good but the country broken, after you enter Mass the hills are longer, the land under better cultivation & more appearances of wealth.

A meeting House in Oxford for Universalists, built about the time of my birth [1791].[3] Farmers are ployed in cutting grass & grain. The former not averaging a half ton—the acre! The latter as good as ever known.

Very much diverted in Burrillville with the Taverner. A sing song sort of man at first sight but very <u>cute</u> withal. He questioned me for the space of 20 minutes in every ingenious way to ascertain my profession etc. etc. in which he must have undoubtly succeeded had I had one to boast of in spite of myself. He is a man of taste & always takes a <u>nap</u> of an afternoon. Wears a whig which does not conceal a very good head of hair. All the family have a nasal twang.

Pray sir do you live on the street,—no—on the hill? Then likely

---

1. Daniel Angell (1777-1860) was a fifth-generation descendant of Thomas Angell, who settled Providence with Roger Williams in 1636. Daniel Angell served five years in the Rhode Island legislature; his tavern, built ca. 1800, was south of the intersection of Douglas Turnpike and Harris Road in the village of Stillwater. The head of an elk, shot by his grandfather and reputedly the last elk killed in Rhode Island, hung in the tavern. The building still stands; it is now a private home.

The Douglas Turnpike, a private toll road chartered by the Rhode Island legislature in 1805, extended "from Providence to the Massachusetts line into the towns of Douglas or Uxbridge."

2. Campbell's Tavern was at the corner of Main and Charlton Streets in Oxford. The first proprietor was Daniel Eliott, about 1714. In 1812 the tavern was purchased from Henry Campbell by his brother, Maj. Archibald Campbell, who ran the establishment until his death in 1818.

3. The Universalist Meeting House was built in 1791 on land leased to the Society by the Campbell Tavern estate.

near Squire Thurbers,[4]—no—may be you keep an office near the market,—no—you belong to the College[5] I suppose,—no—a pause again. Then as you keep a store you can tell me the price of flour? I do not keep a store, sir. Here the poor man's ingenuity ran out & he determined to let me rest. His name Walden.[6]

Not less than half the land in the part of this town I passed uncleared. Rough & poverty stricken tho' some symptoms of improvement.

7th

Move a little after five, pass Charlton and Sturbridge to Rices[7] in Brookfield 17 miles.

Up & down nearly the whole distance. Weather very bad. Country thickly settled, well walled & tolerably improved. Good for grazing grain too looking better than in R.I. Several fields of wheat heavy. Breakfast and lay by 5 hours and a half. Dine whith stage passengers from Boston. Then thro' Western [Brookfield] &

---

4. Squire Thurber (1759-1837) and his brothers operated a blacksmith shop at the foot of Waterman Street in downtown Providence.

5. Rhode Island College, founded in 1764, was renamed Brown University in 1804, but was still referred to locally as "the College." John Brown Francis graduated in 1808 from the institution named for his uncle, Nicholas Brown Jr.

6. John Walden was living in Burrillville by 1810, according to state census records. His tavern, in the Nasonville section of Burrillville at the junction of Douglas Pike and Victory Highway, still stands; it is known today as the Western Hotel. According to Averill Maher, historian and treasurer of the Burrillville Historical Preservation Society, the tavern itself dates to the 1770s and was a stop on the stagecoach route between Providence and Worcester. However, the Rhode Island Historical Preservation Commission dates it to 1805.

7. The Rice homestead was built ca. 1719 by Azariah Rice and still stands. When Francis stayed there, it was owned by the Buckminster Rice family, whose daughter Frances married Hezekiah Sabin of Providence, a cousin and clerk to John Brown, Francis's grandfather. Buckminster Rice's cousin Frank Rice built the popular Golden Ball Tavern in Providence in 1784.

Ware to Belchertown in Hampshire county 30 miles. Tavern kept by Mr. Clapp[8] & a very good one.

8th

Move again a little after five. Air sultry & hotter than yesterday. The wind at my back—dusty. A tolerably level country by comparison to Northampton.

Broom corn in great abundance seen on the bottom land in the neighbourhood of the Connecticut. No enclosure for a distance of two miles from the river & as far along the banks. The Town of Hadley tho't to raise brooms to the annual value of $10,000.—No stone within last 20 or 30 miles. Fences of wood. Good land for grain. A light warm soil. 15 miles [before] breakfast—ride five miles and sup. 3 hours then over [Chesterfield Mountains] to Worthington 16 miles. Obliged to walk the horse. Travel at the rate of three miles the hour & improve every level space between the hills in a brisk jog too!!! It is impossible to do anything more then creep down these mountains & even then the motion of the horse is extremely uncomfortable. The strain on the legs and across the loins always painful.

9th

Advance at five. Cloudy & misty. Resort to a great coat but intolerable hot when the sun appears. Get in 10 miles over the mountains in [pain]—so the old woman toll-keeper[9] says—thank God.

Two miles & one half the hour!!! The last eight miles before reaching Pittsfield. Pleasant travelling. 18 or 20 miles—breakfast at

---

8. James Harvey Clapp (1792-1871) opened the Tavern on South Main Street in Belchertown shortly after his arrival in 1812. He also ran a stagecoach line from Boston to Albany, and served three terms in the Massachusetts legislature.

9. John Brown Francis was traveling over the Third Massachusetts Turnpike (later called the Worthington Turnpike), chartered in 1797, which ran roughly 32 miles from Northampton to Pittsfield. In 1829 it was made a free road.

Center's Coffee House.[10] Very good house in the bargain. Then to New Lebanon—7 miles and lay by.

Not much company. It is a year this day since I come to this place with J.K. Angell.[11] The water has lost none of its virtue for bathing.[12] A bath's worth a ride of an hundred miles to a man of pleasures. The skin is rendered so soft and it is really a luxury to feel of oneself after being soaked in it.

The bath is about waist high & the water runs in at a troth without cessation by removing the little gate at the bottom the bath is emptied. You can then place yourself under this stream from the troth and be most thoroughly cleansed. This sensation is infinately delightful.

At Pittsfield hears a long argument between a dancing master and tape measurer on the utility of dancing. The dancing master talked like a philosopher and might have puzzled a wiser casuist than a tape man—Memo: the first dancing master I have ever met who knew the <u>positions</u> of an argument.

E. Watson[13] moved from this place in the spring reckoned a rich man. Daughter Emily married and gone to Detroit. Farm sold to a

---

10. Ebenezer Center (1768-1822), owner of the coffee house, was a prominent Pittsfield merchant and an incorporator of the Berkshire Bank.

11. J.K. Angell (1794-1857), a graduate of Brown University, class of 1813, was a leading Rhode Island attorney and editor of the *United States Law Intelligences and Review* from 1829 to 1831. One of his most notable publications, still used today, is the *Law of Water Courses and a Treatise on Tide Waters* (1826). In 1820 Angell sailed for London to lay claim to a large British estate he believed he held title to. While there he also acted on behalf of John Brown Francis, who was attempting to recover monies from a lawsuit involving the merchant ship *President Washington*, which belonged to his father John Francis and grandfather John Brown. Both claims ultimately came to naught.

12. The mineral springs at New Lebanon were a popular bathing spot.

13. Elkanah Watson (1758-1842) became an indentured servant to John Brown in 1773, at age 15. When Brown was taken prisoner by Capt. James Wallace of the British ship H.M.S. *Rose* at Newport in 1776, Watson made a dash on horseback to

Bostonian.

N[ew] Y[or]K money current on the west of the CON[necticu]T [River]. The trades of this county exclusively to the N[orth—i.e., Hudson] River. No silver change & a great deal of trouble with their paper facility. The facility looses its name like many other important things out of its own Parish. The traveler therefore must always be on the watch which is something disagreeable.

The country between P[ittsfield] and N[ew] L[ebanon] surpassing any inland scenery in the U.S. This I say without book, prehaps & prehaps not. Hancock's mountain the most difficult for the traveller. Upon an angle of 45° & one mile & one half long. Hancock frontier town of Massachusetts.

Plymouth, Mass. There he obtained two dilapidated fishing schooners, armed with rusty cannons and open barrels of gunpowder, and set off to try to intercept the *Rose* on its way to Boston. Fortunately a confrontation never occurred, and John Brown was eventually set free.

Watson was released from his indenture in 1777. That year, John Brown sent him to Charleston and other southern cities with $50,000 to invest in local cargoes for shipment to Europe. In 1779 he opened a commercial house in Nantes, France, on behalf of John Brown and partners. In later life he owned a farm in Pittsfield, Mass., founded the Berkshire Agricultural Society, and avidly promoted inland navigation by canals. In 1816 he moved to Albany, where he founded the first agricultural society in New York State; he had already worked for some years on the development of the Erie Canal. (See n. 15, Part III.) He eventually published *History of the Western Canals in the State of New York and Agricultural Societies on the Modern Berkshire System*, among other books.

In 1835, while John Brown Francis was Governor of Rhode Island, Watson wrote the following tribute to his former employer, Francis's grandfather:

Port Kent, on Lake Champlain—9th June 1835

Gov. John Brown Francis
In commemoration of the day which bound me by indenture to your enterprising Grandfather, John Brown, 62 years ago and identified me in his family. In gratitude for his paternal care. In affection[ate] recollection of mutual ties of friendship which attached me to your blessed Mother [Abby Brown Francis] in early life. A life full of incidents, mainly devoted in the promotion of public happiness, may be all traced to the example of your departed Grandfather. [Hand-copied letter from J.B. Francis's personal papers.]

10th

Hot again—ride 10 miles to breakfast over good road thro' a poor country to the Hudson, very uneven barren uninteresting.

Albany a great thoroughfare—horses all crowded when the steam boat embowels.

Visited the Treasury department & the comptroller & a money changer.

Then home again to Baird's,[14] a house on a great scale. Met Low of NYK.[15] A facetious fashionable character—on his way to Ballston. Tells bloody stories of the NYK bloods some Bobadils[16] among them no doubt. Many of them would appear as famous for their amoury as Sir Henry Marten[17] of Oliver Cromwell memory—drinking, whoring & gambling the order of the day from all of which good Lord deliver me. The bad effects of hard drink always

---

14. John Baird owned the Eagle Tavern at 493 South Market Street, Albany. Typical menus of the period at such upscale hostelries might include, for breakfast, ham, veal, fish, toast, cucumbers, cheese, preserved apples, gingerbread, shortcake, salad and coffee. Dinner would be even more lavish, e.g., fish, roast beef, boiled lamb, broiled chicken, potatoes, squash, beetroot, green cabbage, pickled cucumbers, cold and melted butter, apple pie, cheese, and pudding.

15. Nicholas Low (1739-1826), born in New Brunswick, N.J., was a Federalist delegate to the Constitutional Convention in 1788-89. In 1795 Low and others purchased a 300,000-acre tract in the Adirondacks from William Constable and established the town of Lowville. Between 1800 and 1810 he purchased land in Saratoga County at Ballston Spa, renowned for its mineral waters, and built a hotel and a cotton factory there.

16. Boabdil was the last Moorish king of Granada, whose dramatic life gave rise to a number of romantic legends. After seizing the throne from his father in 1482 and plunging Granada into civil war, he secretly treatied with the Castilian Christians who were launching their own attack on the kingdom, then reneged and fought valiantly against them. Forced to surrender in January 1492, he fled to Morocco, ending centuries of Moorish rule in southern Spain.

17. Henry Marten (1602-1680), member of Parliament and a supporter of Oliver Cromwell, was a notorious rake who squandered a large inheritance on pretty women and high living King Charles called him "an ugly rascal and a whore-

outweigh the delerium. Tho' prehaps a slight degree of elevation is desirable but then it can't be kept up without deeper draughts & here comes the difficulty.

A second species of dissipation viz. a taste for common women: Ex[?] as can be so much against my stomach that I never could think highly of the man who followed them. The morality of the thing in an unmarried man is not to be regarded a pins head.

The third offence is prehaps worse than all the rest. I like cards but shall never fall to gambling because so many coil passions are awakened that the enjoyment is suspended.

11th

Had not resolution to encounter a thick fog before breakfast & then more was required to withstand a scorching sun over the infernal road between A[lbany] and Schenectady.

The country looking worse than ever—literally like a country in mourning, the shrub pine having been burnt to coal, thro' accident I suppose—never enquired. The taverns multiply on this road but no one except a Tavern Keeper would consent to inhabit such a country. Nature however must have intended it for something, for nature is but art unknown to thee & says the philosopher it remains for the ingenuity of man but I very much doubt whether any use will be found for this extensive wilderness of Pine any sooner than Mr. Redheffer's perpetural motion [machine].[18] When water runs

---

master." After Cromwell appointed him a judge, however, Marten had the last word, signing the death warrant that led to Charles's beheading in 1649.

18. In the early 19th century, a man named Redheffer claimed to have discovered the elusive secret of the perpetual motion machine. He traversed the United States showing his contraption, which ran by a system of weights and counter-weights that appeared to keep the wheels in constant motion. It was a convincing enough performance that Redheffer was trumpeted to the world as the man who had finally solved the great problem. But the American inventor Jacob Perkins (1766-1849) examined the machine and saw that its visible mechanisms were

up hill or as Potter says a man can lift himself up by his own ears, then will perpetural motion, or the use of [a sand] barren or some other equally <u>outre</u> thing discover itself.

Lodge at Outh—In Amsterdam, Montgomery County—the largest in the State, much larger than the State of R.I.

15 miles from S[chenectady], road rough, the [land] flat as far as this, very narrow along the river—not averaging twenty rods.

The landlady very civil tells a long story of the depravity of her countrymen. 10 men now on jail at Johnson—all natives hereabouts & a hundred more in the gang. No end to their robberies.

Accommodating People.

12th

The room being dark & the people not calling me did not ride till six then rode at the rate of 5 1/4 miles the hour, 23 miles without stopping. The first good day for travelling I have had. The dust laid & a fresh breeze in my face. The mare performing to the admiration of every body I meet. Asked her age more than four times this morn'g—.

The flat land wider but said to be wearing out by incessant irrigation without manure. Crop after crop & very few cattle kept will bring any bottom[land] low in a space of one or two hundred years.

The Germans[19] sole inhabitants—all rich lazy & ignorant. Their skulls as impenetrable as the Congo race.

---

inadequate to produce the results it showed. His mechanical knowledge enabled him to detect the corner of the machine through which a hidden power source kept it moving, and he confidently declared, "Pass a saw through that post, and your perpetual motion will stop." Redheffer refused to put his machine to the test, but it was afterwards discovered that a cord passed down through the post into the cellar, where a man was stationed to restore the weights at each revolution.

19. Most German settlers in the upper Mohawk Valley prior to the American Revolution came originally from the Rhine Valley in the Lower Palatinate region

40 bushels of corn said to be average crop, but I doubt grain in this part of the world never so scarce before—gave landlady 1 Dr [dollar] for a half bushel of oats!!

Timber along the Mohawk chiefly butternut, basswood, elm and walnut—no underbrush.

The Dutch go from one age to another without any variation in their modes of cultivation. Their horses fat but cows & other stock starved in the winter. They are very wealthy but few of them can be pursuaded to loan money on interest, it is generally locked up.

The instrument to cut grain is peculiar to them. A small scythe wielded by the right hand, the <u>schysher</u> as he is called slashed along without much labor apparently & as the grain falls pulls it oneside with a small hook in his left hand. This is called <u>scything</u> instead of mowing. Never saw finer fields of grain. Lodged at the Little Falls. Finks—good house—20 miles from Utica and 43 miles from Amsterdam. Travelled the last ten miles with a Presbyterian clergyman. Had a long controversy with him about Popery and Infidels. Amused at his style of reasoning or his want of reason when taken from the supernatural ground—like Billy Harding he proposed his divinty books but his jaws locked when I told him that my theory had no relation to theology. He seemed to think with all of his trade that every question of policy which must of necessity change with everything else could be settled only by the writings of these wool gathering divines of the last century. Alas poor human nature has forcibly the idea of W.R. presents itself that most people take up

---

of Germany—hence the name Palatines by which they were known. Many had fled to Holland to escape the Thirty Years' War (1618-48) and later accepted the sanctuary offered by the Protestant Queen Anne of England. Of the 30,000 who came from Holland to London, roughly 4,000 became part of England's plan to settle the American colonies and make them revenue producing. Many arrived in the New World in June of 1710, settling first in the upper Hudson Valley and later in the Schoharie Valley and Mohawk River region.

their opinions on trust & may be said to borrow rather than beget their ideas.

Met with the first man besides Low who has known me & him I did not recollect.

Fell in with a boy from R.I.—name Harris tells me Judge Bowen[20] has been considered out of his head. Quere: would the Bowens acknowledge this? The poor devil probably always had less head to boast of than any of his family & their natural parts were never of the first rate, as Cousin Obadiah[21] might say.

13th

Breakfast & rode 7 miles to the village of Herkimer the county town of our tract not less than a hundred miles off. Tell it not in oath—galloped into Utica 16 miles.

There are fewer locust trees both in this state and Mass. where I have passed than in R.I. The few I have seen however are not as with us, afflicted with the worm. The leaf larger, the body more smooth and tho' a handsome tree anywhere much more so here.

Called to see Ballou[22] and drank tea. His wife an amiable fine little woman destined to be pinched and live in fear of poverty all her days, one of the most cruel of all doubtful cases tho' not as bad Othello would say as one who dotes yet doubts suspect but

---

20. Judge Jabez Bowen (1739-1815) married Sarah, daughter of Obadiah Brown (see n. 21). He served as Chancellor of Brown University, Deputy Governor of Rhode Island and Judge of the Rhode Island Superior Court.

21. Obadiah Brown (1762-1815) was the son of Joseph, second eldest of the four brothers (John, Joseph, Nicholas, and Moses) who founded the Brown dynasty in Providence. He was thus John Brown Francis's first cousin once removed. A partner in the firm of Brown, Rogers and Brown, Obadiah was a lifelong bachelor with a reputation as a freethinker

22. Joseph Ballou, a commercial agent who sold food and supplies to local settlers, moved from Exeter, R.I. to Utica in 1792 with his wife and three children. He acquired much land in Utica, selling four acres to Moses Bagg (see n. 4, Part III).

strongly loves, Heaven defend her from this addition to her calamities.

Ballou has been really poor but from his obstinacy in holding on to land when it was reasonable as every one thought for him to sell & disembarrass himself & the unexpected rise in value of this property he is now in reality rich, but the same obstinacy remains & he refuses to sell & goes on encumbered with debt, starving his family & knowing that the same adverse fluctuation in this village will again entangle & overwhelm him. What strange infatuation I called him a fool & a jackal & by every hard name but he'll sit like the teamster with his waggon in the mud waiting for Hercules to draw him out. He'll suffer his wife & children to pine amidst his store & run the hazard of having them beggars. For leave them he will before many years in a consumption but not before the fictitious value of lots in this village is over & their hopes past redemption. There has been a singular fall of land into the Canada Creek this season. Six or eight acres are said to have tumbled in or thro' the bed of the stream. There are instances of this sort on record I believe. In Switzerland villages have been covered up by the giving way of mountains. How it is accounted for I do not know.

14th
Yesterday afternoon & this day employed in looking about <u>dangling my watch knot </u>and reading extracts from the manuscript book,—lifes a dream—tis all a delusion prehaps.

15th
Another sultry day. Trenton 13 miles. Lodge at Fowler's in Remsen. A wretched phlegm cutter on the borders of the wood. Raining hard & threating a storm. Found no letters at the Post office & feeling like a cut throat go to bed. The confusion & vulgarity of the bar room enough to sicken one with plebian manners.

16th

The morn'g pleasant. The news of my arrival [in Boonville] has given the Bar Keeper more than his usual custom from mere curiosity or the desires of hearing from R.I. A mob had collected. My horse was to be admired, my motions watched & everything attended to with that sort of scrupulosity which people in low life on the confines of a wilderness might be supposed to entertain towards the proprietor of a neighbouring Tract of Land—the only property of which they have any conception. If say one I am well off with a lot of one hundred acres & log hut what may be said to his situation with one hundred thousand acres.

How true the doctrines that every heart knows its own bitterness. These people are disposed to call in question the justice of that disease which makes them hewers of wood and drawers of water & leaves me to consume only but little do they think that the most unfortunate of their clan has fewer moments of care. Less concern about the future than the object of their envy. A being who has discovered at the early age of twenty five that almost everything in this life is flat, stale, & unprofitable & that there is scarcely anything worth living for. A sort of knowledge which is better learned at an hour when mortality puts on immortality—an idea indeed that would be more impressed if men were less in dread of falling into naught, it is this alone that peoples the earth, & makes us rather bear those ills we know than fly to those we know not of.

The man who is planted at Beaver Meadow, 12 miles in the woods insisted on accompaning me for he wanted as he said to talk <u>sentiment to me.</u> I could not help exclaiming. Even the wilderness then is no defence against these sentamentalists if I escape the verbiage of pious, pedantic, lifeless, sapless declaimers of one sex I am to be pursued to the very mouth of my cave by a satellite of the opposite gender.

Good Lord deliver me. I saw the storm gathering however & prepared for it. In other words I guarded myself against a sermon from this long winded, wiskey drinking Hall by dosing him with his favorite beverage till his ideas could no longer get utterance & then we rode to his chanty very peaceably not meeting a living thing—man or beast. His wife boiled me eggs as hard as a rock before I thought of giving direction. The poor woman had sent out for materials & actually made pies for me several times expecting my arrival. She was inconsolable at not having the power to treat me with venison or trout & insisted on my stay over night but confident that I could struggle thro' to the settlement proceeded.

The road damnable it made my heart ake to press the poor animal thro' mire & over stumps & stones, where her legs were in so much danger of being broken. The bridges & logways were worse than all. I found myself obliged to dismount & actually stand in front of the poor devil to prevent her from precipitating herself into the gulphs. Before I did this she gave a spring over a place where those logs had rotted & fallen & I went through with her hind legs as they came on the opposite sides.

By a singular effort she extricated herself without the slightest contusion.

At Moose River the bridge being gone, was obliged to ford the river. Here my spurs were necessary after several incissions up to the [gravel] head, she sprang from the bank at one leap into the stream. The water was not above her shoulders. In 6 miles I alighted at Betsy Vincent's[23] who came to receive me in the attitude of suckling her babe. One she seemed to have chosen on the occasion—certainly the most interesting situation for tho' our women would shudder at the idea of exposing a breast but their chastity or delicacy is no greater than Betsy's, a very honest hearted communicative well meaning interesting little woman. This her first child. She described her sufferings from a broken

---

23. Elizabeth (Betsy) Joy Vincent was the daughter of Maj. Abiathai Joy (see n. 27) and wife of Nicholas Vincent. They were the first couple to be married on Brown's Tract.

breast. Women certainly endure pain better than men.

Remounted crossed the river & found Mr. H[erreshoff][24] grinding his coffee. All glad to see me—at least they say so, I have no reason to doubt their sincerity.

17th

Fine summer weather, the thermometer at 70 in the morn'g. The late frosts had injured the potatoes, Wheat looking well where it took seed but the greater part poorly seeded or prehaps winter killed. The rye always good here. One field of about 12 acres—surpassing any crop I ever saw. Thirty bushels to the acre undoubtly. Some of the ears on measurement not less than seven feet from the earth.

Who can talk of the impracticability of settling a country where the yield is so abundant & the climate so healthy—absurd.

The old Hunter White hearing of my arrival brought a mess of trout. He had killed seven Beavers within the last week. The skins of which averaged 12 Dr. each in value. His success in fishing this season equally remarkable.

An old hump backed dwarf is now on the lake living on hard

---

24. Charles Frederick Herreshoff (1769-1819) was born Carl Friedrich Herreschoff in Minden, Germany, immigrated to America in 1787, and in 1801 married John Brown Francis's aunt Sarah, daughter of John Brown. Herreshoff first visited John Brown's 210,000-acre tract in Herkimer and Lewis Counties in 1811, and eventually acted as family agent to settle the wild lands along the Black River. A true pioneer in North Country development, he cleared over 2,000 acres, built bridges, and constructed a forge for processing iron ore and turning it into bar iron and finished nails. In 1817 he invented a unique device for separating iron ore from rock (described in Part III of the diary). But the solitary, Sisyphean task of taming such an inhospitable country and making it profitable, and the shame he felt at his difficulty extricating himself from debt, eventually overwhelmed him. He committed suicide December 19, 1819 at what is now Thendara, N.Y., leaving his wife and five children in Bristol, R.I.

rye bread & water & after six weeks steady tiltuping[25] boasts of half a barrel of salmons trout. A quantity which White would have certainly caught in some number of hours.

18th

This poor dwarf made his entrance today looking as greasy as a bear. He thinks himself in a fair way of getting rich—tho' he has caught scarcely fish enough to pay for his hard bread, he comes for a fresh supply. The fool is happy that he knows no more. He took the very worst time to come to the mill—in a very high wind being in the middle of the lake and afraid to encounter a side sea he was obliged to paddle in the eye of the wind. This poor deformed wreach something in the shape of Sir Hudibras[26] tho' of smaller dimensions not being over four and one half feet has married his punctual dose of wives. His third is now alive. It would puzzle a casuist to account for the choice of these women to be sure. A man should never suffer himself to be flattered by the love of a woman when it is dependent on no standard of taste, no principle of virtue nor any criteria whatsoever. Pride aside & the devil alone could guess her fantasies.

Went to see Betsy today & cheer her in her affliction. Then to her mothers & the old Lady Grandmother Joy 90 years old, a well

---

25. A term for camping outdoors, from "tilt-up," meaning a tent or other collapsible cover.

26. *Hudibras* was a satirical poem by the 17th-century English poet Samuel Butler, published in three parts between 1663 and 1678, that attacked the hypocrisy and pedantry of the Puritans. Modeled on Don Quixote, the poem's hero is a caricature of Butler's patron Sir Samuel Luke, one of Cromwell's officers. Sir Hudibras, a fat hunchback, sallies forth on an old nag with Ralpho (his Sancho Panza) to put the world to rights and especially to stop people from enjoying themselves. They spend much of their time quarreling over trivial theological points.

bred, mild, ancient lass. The Major[27] & his promising son Miatha at work on my road with six others. The daughter Susan handsome—about 17 years. Millee as they call her, an old maid, a rare character in a new country, her age twenty five only tho' she has been rated in the old maids row these two years. She has met with losses no doubt, for no true woman was ever voluntarily an old maid, it is an unnatural state.

Cole the man who is clearing fifty acres for Mr. H[erreshoff] arrived today with a gang of hands & a woman to <u>serve</u>, as Betsy shrewdly suspects, as women serve in camps, the mistress of the company. Well done Betsy—A cow two horses & one yoke of oxen compose the retinue i.g.—good weather in the morn'g. Sent for Major Joy to abandon his road for the present & wait my return from Boonville. He answered summons immediately. Hear of the loss of the barn at the middle settlement by fire which is a damage of a cool five hundred to me. Joy the unintentional cause.

20th

A cool blustering day—put on another pair of pantaloons & in the afternoon build a fire!!!

Major Joy brings a Captain Pringle to see me. A man who wants a task on my road & applies for the Clarks lot, meaning as he says to move on here, family not hostile. Send a letter by him to Stephen Smith the Surveyor to meet me at Boonville Monday morn'g the 26th instant prepared to cross the Black River & explore a route to Moose River.

Pringle engaged as chainman.[28]

---

27. Maj. Abiathai Joy (1762-1851), born in Rehoboth, Mass., served in Capt. Blakeslee's Vermont unit in the Revolutionary War. He moved to Remsen, N.Y., ca. 1803. In 1814 he bought 160 acres near Herreshoff's forge (see n. 24).

28. Chains 66 feet long (containing 100 links) were used to measure distances when surveying; thus a "chainman" was a surveyor's helper.

21st

Joy kept me in the house all morn'g on a consultation about his whipping Mrs. Clarke. Advised him not to let the affair go to Court. The woman was <u>enceinte</u> & a damned bitch undoubtably but no man is justified in my opinion in striking a woman but in a case se defendendo. The law however authorizes the chastisement of a common scold by the proper officer & of the <u>wholesome</u> chastisement of ones wife. The poor devil is to be pitied who has a wife that needs such regulation.

There should be an entire reciprocity of interests & feelings. But this supposes <u>mind</u> on both sides. An amiable & sensible tho' not a learned woman will always escape unkind treatment if her husband has not a boists [?] or has any principle of humanity—in his composition.

Ice was seen this morn'g about the houses for the first time since <u>the ninth of July</u>!! [29] A large fire put our comfort again—This would be a most excellent place for a studious character: a winters residence would convert me.

I forgot to observe that White shot a Deer yesterday as he said tho' Cole found & consumed it on the presumption that a wolf had destroyed the poor animal. W bro't me the tenderloin but it proved a damn tough loin—hung it down the well.[30]

Parker the Dwarf left this [day] on another expedition with nothing but hard bread, it would really [seem] as was said in another case he was doing God a service to put such a miserable

---

29. Following the catastrophic eruption in 1815 of Mt. Tambora in Indonesia, 1816 came to be known as the "year without summer." The dust and ash expelled into the upper atmosphere lowered the global temperature an average of one degree Fahrenheit. In the U.S., the Northeast harvested less than a fourth of the corn sown, and there were serious shortages of food in New York, Philadelphia, and Boston. The Adirondack region normally has fewer than three frost-free months in a year, so its already short growing season was cut even shorter in 1816.

30. Hanging game down a well kept it out of reach of predators.

apology of a man out of fortunes power. In other words to knock him in the head.

22nd
We expected a hard frost this morn'g but fog saved us.

A man from Remsen today—a great religious stir there which he attributes "to the cold snap." All Methodists they fall by the dozens he says but always on their bottoms.[31] These Methodists have their run at intervals as much in this country as in England. Religion goes by fits & starts, as one sheep leads a whole flock over a wall so one or two conversions sanctifies a leash of gossips. They are as wild & mobocratic as in Cromwells time & only want the power to do the same mischief.

A plague on this influence of priestcraft—I say.

Mr. H[erreshoff] concludes to go out with me tomorrow—

Boonville, Oneida County
Aug 27th
In company with Smith the Surveyor & three pack men crossed the Black river to explore & mark a route for a road to our settlement. We forded the river but the stones being slippery & my shoes fell off, fell in & bruised my ankle.

The land at first excellent but timber not of the same quality as on the opposite shore. Land rising gradually & afterwards in ridges till we descended a precepice & ran in a gulph for three hours making little progress. On regaining good ground Smith & myself left

---

31. In 1802 the Rev. John Taylor of Deerfield, Mass., did a "missionary tour" by horseback and stagecoach through the Mohawk and Black River region. Taylor, who was probably a Congregationalist, wrote disapprovingly of how the Methodists in church would "fall down...and, after lying twenty or thirty minutes, rise, crying glory to God. Some of them appeared to be senseless—others in great agitation." [O'Callaghan, *History*, v. 3, pp. 1113-4.]

the party & found a course to the right. On the south of the gulph as smooth as a house floor.

Then on the same kind of land covered with hard timber a little more than three miles & an half & night coming on obliged to chanty without water—a serious evil—no one can be aware of the disappointment who has not felt as I now feel. We have built an excellent chanty, the spruce pealing easily; the rain pours at this moment but it does not leak. Men employed in cutting wood & breaking hemlock boughs for a bed—soaking wet.

Nothing but salt pork & poor bread & whiskey—hard fare by the Lord. I write now by the light of a tremendous fire—a flaming Etna. Men weary & faint hearted—feel well myself physically but had rather be at home.

Smith examining my watch seal & wanting to know what is on it.[32] [He asked] "Was I where that came from."

28th

It cleared & we saw stars at one o'clock. The men waked me from a profound sleep insisting upon it—it was morn'g. My watch made them quiet again. All hands complain of cold. The frost must have been severe. No complaint from hard fare. Caught no water in our kettle. Moved as soon as we could see & breakfasted on the outside of a dismal swamp. Chocolate & sugar hardly palatable.

The course supposed good at the right. Suffer from cold—all hands complain. After getting through the swamp one hundred rods on level land again. Smith goes off & finds a course round this deviltry to the right. This if true makes our route superior to any one ever run in a broken country.

Returned from the excursion the last day of August—having followed back the tally line where it was good & diverted from it

---

32. A watch seal, often engraved with the wearer's family crest, hung from the watch fob and was used to seal wax on letters and documents.

where it was not. By this means obtained an excellent route—for miles as level as a house floor. Little is to be said in favor of it however in the vicinity of Moose river country thereabouts as wild as the stream itself which from this circumstance is the most interesting stream I ever saw. We struck it in eight miles & 16 chains on a course from B[lack] River on No 5 Adgate Tract North 45 degrees east. The second day at four o'clk then crossed & crawled along the banks & thro' deviltry of every kind till night, in search of my grandfather's [John Brown's] old clearing.

The Surveyor fearful of having made some error prehaps, was for pushing farther but I peremptorily ordered the men to lay down their packs & build a chanty tho' the light from the river might have enabled us to see much later than usual, but we were all just dead with fatigue & the night required a roaring fire. Never slept better.

In the morn'g concluded to go to the three miles trail by the old line but crossed without perceiving it & walked over the <u>damndest</u> of all countries up hill & thro' swamp till 1/2 past 11 o'clk. I fearful the whole time too that this wretched country was a part of my inheritance till we were arrested by the roaring of a river which we immediately ran to & found to our astonishment one of which, no one had any knowledge.33 After taking breakfast for we had started without it on the plan of finding [Major] Joy on his road & getting milk for our chocolate. In the belief that it must be a branch of M[oose] River & that none of the country we had traversed was mine but the dead Frenchmans34 & therefore to the south of

---

33. The unknown river was apparently the South Branch of the Moose River.

34. Pierre Pharoux, a brilliant architect and engineer, came to America to act as agent for theCompagnie de New York. Paul Chassanis and Jacques LeRay (see n. 12, Part III) bought land on the Oswego River in 1793 from William Constable (see n. 53), naming it Castorland and forming the Compagnie to oversee its development. Despite boundary disputes with Constable, Pharoux's efforts to develop Castorland seemed promising. But in 1795, while rafting on the Black River, Pharoux was swept over the Great Falls (now Lyons Falls) to his death.

B[rown] T[ract] I gave S[mith] my compass & told him to steer W & then a little North. This course bro't us where we desired. Found Joy—took some of his boiled pork & beans—a great treat for dinner & with him ran a line for Moose river from the 5 mile tree. Hit it at the fall below the old clearing.

The next day surveyed a place for [a] bridge then took the men one half mile above the clearing to a rocky island practical for a bridge. From there struck for the old line again & from the 5 1/2 mile tree on high ground struck for this Island. Then ran up—found a better place still. Crossed & ran W 45° N—The rain fell, the route was bad & the air shivery. Struck the old road in 1/2 a mile. I followed & I took his direction from my voice—this to avoid crooks—his course was horrid—mine quite tolerable. Made a chanty in about two miles & one half—wet to the skin. It poured but we were secure—never slept better. In the morn'g obliged to cut my boots & even then two men could hardly wrench them. No person should walk the woods in boots.

Our line from this chanty or rather the old one altered—capital!

Recrossed Black River the water having risen waist high. I had reserved a private flask of brandy to swig after this baptising but lost it all in taking it from my pocket. This one of the miseries of human life unquestionably. The river two miles & upward from the tavern. Walked quickly & sufferd no inconvenience.

1st Sept

Major Joy agreeable to [his] promise this morn'g appeared with two letters—one from M.B.I. [Moses Brown Ives]35 & another from

---

35. Moses Brown Ives (1794-1857) was a cousin of John Brown Francis, with whom he attended Judge Tapping Reeves's law school in Litchfield, Conn. (see n. 9, p. 69). In 1832 he became a partner in the Providence mercantile firm of Brown & Ives. One of the city's leading men, he was president of the Providence Bank, a founder of the Providence Athenaeum, a supporter of Butler Hospital, and a founder of Rhode Island Hospital.

the Matthew Coxe Lane. God knows how grateful they were to me. Home is home or the old saying goes if ever so homely.

Rode this day to Lowville. The country more settled as you follow the river. Had a view of the people in their go to meeting clothes as I passed Martinsburg when I saw the first house of God. Not such a one 'tis to be hoped as Sir Hudibras describes where they never built a house of prayer but the devil had his chapel there.

There is so much to be said about Lowville that I forbear saying anything. The part of my time spent here will be remembered but as I am not good at recollecting names let me put them down.

Judge Stow[36] late a mem[ber] of Congress—a giant of a man & very agreeable one. His conversation every the character of Mr. Mason[37] only he is better read in scriptures & possesses more

---

36. Judge Silas Stow (1773-1827) was born in Middlefield, Conn., studied law, and in 1797 was appointed by Nicholas Low (see n. 15) as agent for his Black River tract. One of the first settlers of Lowville, he built a large mansion that overlooked the settlement and donated a parcel of land for the construction of a meeting house, which in 1808 became the first site of Lowville Academy. Stow served in Congress as a Federalist from 1811 to 1813, and was the first judge of Lewis County.

37. James Brown Mason (1774/75-1819) was born in Connecticut, graduated from Rhode Island College in 1791 and studied medicine and surgery. In 1799 his courtship of Alice Brown, youngest daughter of John and Sarah Brown, resulted in Alice becoming pregnant shortly after her father left for Philadelphia to serve as a Federalist representative in Congress. When he returned to Providence, John Brown was well aware of his daughter's condition, but refused to allow her to wed Mr. Mason. As her confinement approached, however, their marriage must have seemed the lesser evil, for a private wedding ceremony was performed by the Rev. Stephen Gano on July 16, 1800. The following day Alice gave birth to a daughter, Abby Mason (John Brown Francis's first cousin). James Brown Mason went on to become a prominent businessman and citizen, serving as trustee of Brown University, major general of the Rhode Island Militia, a two-term member of Congress, executor of his father-in-law's estate, and agent for the Brown heirs in the development of John Brown's Tract. He died August 31, 1819, four months before his brother-in-law Charles Herreshoff's suicide.

humour.

Next Bostwick[38] the great land agent naturally eloquent, enthusiastic & fond of company too. The most violent man I ever met—a violent religionist & a violent swearer & drinker sometimes according to ill report—but withal a very pleasant companion for it is amusing to meet with this sort of irrationality if it is only in a transient acquaintanceship.

Then comes Fowler[39] the son of a rich man in NYK of that name—a wild youth of great dispositions—a true Irishman. He is infinately diverting having at command the celebrated passages of Shakespeare & other popular plays, with the talent of mimicry to a G. Cooke[40] in <u>Sir Pertinax</u> he imitates better than Bily & he is Cooper Duff or anybody he pleases.

After him Collins the Lawyer.[41] Cool & Subtle—a cursed dem-

---

38. Isaac Welton Bostwick (1776-1857), a native of Watertown, Conn., was admitted to the bar of the New York Supreme Court in 1801. He moved to Lowville in 1806, formed a law partnership with Samuel Talcott, and succeeded Judge Stow (see n. 37) as land agent for Nicholas Low. Bostwick served as first president of the Lowville Bank and was a supporter and trustee of Lowville Academy, donating 500 volumes to its library.

39. The Macomb Purchase was divided into 27 townships of roughly 32,000 acres apiece, which were numbered and named. The name of Theodosius Fowler, one of the purchasers, was given to township no. 15, but no biographical information has come to light about Fowler, other than what Francis refers to here.

40. George Cooke (1756-1812) was a celebrated English actor, known almost as much for his alcoholism as for his great talent. In 1810-12 he made a grand tour of America, playing to packed houses. John Brown Francis saw him perform in Providence as Sir Pertinax Sycophant in *The Man of the World*, as Shylock in *The Merchant of Venice*, Richard III, Macbeth, Lear, and Falstaff. After Cooke's last performance in Providence in September 1812, he was overcome by the effects of his alcoholism; he died later that month in New York City. A monument to him at the corner of Broadway and Vesey Street bears the inscription: "Three kingdoms claim his birth, Both Hemispheres pronounce his worth."

41. Ela Collins (b. 1786) read law at the offices of Gold & Sill in Whitesboro, N.Y., and began practicing law in Lowville in 1809. He was elected to the General

ocrat in grain. Their unsuccessful Candidate for Congress by 28 votes—but tho' a little precise, a desirable intimate—for he plays whist & becomes liberal among the Romans.

Major Welles the Tavern Keeper binds up the knot. A clever man who knows how to enter into the spirit of his guests & furnish a good table—venison, beef, vegetables, & &. There are others on the outskirts but behind the counter men. My situation confined in a Tavern with such characters & knowing no one else may be imagined.

I have not mentioned Doctor Bradford who as a man & prehaps a companion on a long run I prefer to all & yet he poor man tho' a skillful practioner, is not an economist of consequence goaded with debt. Alas how unaccountable are the desires of fortune. His wife an amiable little woman has no children.

Stow's wife a high toned lady from Boston. Bostwick's wife high toned but a cursed shrew. He took her a pennyless girl of sixteen, he being then a bachelor of thirty five & placed her at the boarding school in Litchfield,[42] after a year or two instruction, married. Domestic tranquility was of short duration between such choleric disposition[s], his irritability heightened too by brandy. She never left his house or rather he turned her out of doors but matters were afterwards compromised. He has now forsworn brandy & takes nothing worse than wine.

Mr. Beach[43] from Watson Tract was also an inmate at the tavern—a very companionable generous soul—too much so for a needy settler. He is a man of more cultivation than any laboring

---

Assembly in 1814, appointed district attorney for Lewis, Jefferson, and St. Lawrence counties in 1815, and elected to Congress in 1822.

42. The Litchfield (Conn.) Female Academy was founded in 1792, and counted Harriet Beecher Stowe among its graduates.

43. John Beach, agent for the Watson Tract, later acted as agent for Brown's Tract as well.

man I ever met & more of a gentleman in his manners. I tremble for him—his tastes & station in life are so much at variance. Whiskey will bring him up—Beach a great disputant. It was divirting to hear him & Bostwick on religious matters.

Beach unhappy—

Fowler rode with me to Beach's house on Watson Tract. The neatest log house I was ever in. His wife as clever as usual, as remarkable for a woman as he for a man.

On our way saw a large Bear who escaped as fast as such a clumsy animal could.

Fowler gained our acquaintance. The Town of which he is proprietor & where he lives was named after him last winter.

He has [a] son illegetimate child by a <u>Black</u> woman living in this house!! A great pet in the family but he never notices it tho' he has been compelled to pay its board. He having the child in the first instance by a Black, argues against his taste & lets him down in my graces. & the studious neglect of the child proves a sort of stoicism beyond my comprehension.

Of any mother a <u>nullius fillius</u> would be an unacceptable presentation.

[Page torn out]

Our intercourse of such a nature must of necessity be transient & if there is any gratification in it then must be sentiment interest & this feeling is destined to every unpleasant trial—you see an object in whose society the most delightful hours are passed continually on the brink of a precipice & you know that all must be sacrificed at last—a painful state of apprehension & one that I shall never again add to the list of my troubles—

So much by way of elegy over poor F[owler] to prevent whose fate I have perhaps unadvisedly exposed myself & literally provoked the attacks of the horde of character mongres.

It is the best act of my life & suffer the most—Justice lays not on this side heaven.

5th Sept.
This day arrived in Boonville & found myself beset by road & bridge jobbers. The fame of my road having spread over the whole country. I was received with great civility as the grandson of old John Brown who is esteemed in these parts, a greater man even than I think Frederick the Great. A thousand questions have been asked, a thousand stories told of this honored grandfather for my diversion. Nothing would satisfy them that he was not also the richest man in the Country & that I myself am not <u>weighed</u> down in the same manner. Every imposition therefore is legalized according to their morality for a rich man is always fair game when one appears it is what the boys call scrambling & it requires the watchfulness of a weasel.

Sept 7th
In Company with Capt. Schuyler the good natured well meaning money getting Store Keeper of old standing, set off for Russia. Left the Capt. & the state road at Remsen village turning to the left arrived at Smiths, twenty five miles a little before dark. His wife a tall brawny squint eyed Methodist & strange to say not the last woman either that my taste would shudder at <u>baiting</u> her methodism.

She sent one of the children for Smith who received my directions & I then rode back to Williams a thriving tavern keeper & whiskey maker

In the morn'g rode to Capt Prindle obtained his terms for making a road between Black & Moose Rivers about 10 1/2 miles & there to Trenton—6 miles.

8th Sunday
Called on Col. Mappa[44] the agent for the Adgate Tract. His salary

---

44. Col. Adam Mappa (d. 1828) was a Dutch exile who had fought against the House of Orange and expatriated himself after the revolution of 1786. He settled

$2400 per annum & his Sons $500 all for a mere bagatelle, he acknowledged to me that he had not sold a lot for the last two years. His sole business then must have been to pay taxes & prevent tresspassers on timber!! This he & his son got nearly $3000!! Alas the stupidity of Dutchmen—his house the best I have seen since I left Utica. He has a daughter of about 18 & a maiden sister. A very courteous old gentleman but strangely ignorant of that part of the tract east of the river. Told him better things but Dutchmen do not take quick. He trembled at the tax I threatened him with.

In the afternoon returned to Boonville.

9th
Bridge builders again got more information about bridges then I ever expected to have—nothing like practice.

10th
Wrote to Prindle offering 12-1/2 Dolls. He to cut, smooth & clear out between the two rivers, one rod in width & wait for his money until it was receivable from the Treasury office agreable to the act appointing me commissioner.

Concluded this day too a contract with Asa Dibble & Jared Ives to construct two bridges such as described in the contract filed among my papers. One over the Black & the other over the Moose River to be completed in the month of Nov. & paid for when the assessment before referred to becomes due, the first for three Hundred Dollars, the second for two hundred & fifty—see agree-

---

first in New Jersey for six years, then moved to Trenton, N.Y. with his family in 1794. He became agent for the Holland Land Company's 45,000-acre Adgate Patent, which had been surveyed by Gerrit Boon, another employee of the Dutch and founder of the successful settlement at Boonville. Upon Mappa's death, the remaining unsold land and assets of the Adgate Tract were purchased by Abraham Varrick, who sold them in turn to Charles A. Mann in 1833.

ment.

Capt. Schuyler agrees to subscribe thirty dollars towards it & advances the money now with twenty more—say fifty on con [dition] that the first thirty be restored in case the bridge is not built or is carried away before May next. The remainder to be refunded in cash for the road [clearing]. Ives & Dibble warrant the bridges until May.

If I have not made a good bargain with these men it is not because I did not understand as much of the business as themselves.

11th

Rec'd letters today from Eliza[45] & Mr. Shearmon. E anticipates a return to P[hiladelphia] when the old Doctor dies. This information disappoints me tho' I ought to have known before that a City woman was always a City woman. I expected something more from Eliza. What woman accustomed to Society & fond of admiration will ever be satisfied with a Country life. This question has agitated me a thousand times & I tho't Eliza one—but where shall I find one now? In Prov? Rochfoucault[46] prehaps settles the point when he says the man deceives himself when he flatters himself exempt from the partialities or frailties that characterize certain situations. There are not exceptions.—Here me miserable. I could point to one if I had not this standard case before me but that person has never like E been given up to the world, she may pos-

---

45. Eliza's identity has never been conclusively determined, but she was the daughter of a prominent Philadelphia doctor—possibly Dr. Owen Wister, whose family had close ties to the Francis family.

46. Francois, duc de la Rochefoucauld (1613-1680) spent much of his life in literary pursuits. In 1665 he published *Maxims and Moral Reflections,* a collection of 360 epigrams which was regarded both as a clear perception of the corruption and hypocrisy of his time and as a model of French prose.

sibly therefore despise it.

I went this day with two men to fix a route from the village to the river. Found a very good one & Mr. Owens blazed the trees. The whole distance varies but little from two miles thro' the woods, but nearly all level & as handsome land as any country can boast. One man has determined to put him up a hut at the river immediately, this may be a great accommodation, it looks well at any rate. I can't help having great hopes of the east side in the neighbourhood of the river, whatever I may think of our Tract—but the nearer the settlement to us the better, sans doute.

Schuyler has promised me to build a mill on the river next season. This of itself will draw people on the east side—only let us have the swing & impulse.

12th - 13th

Rainy weather—sent to Smith to come to me—but 'tis not probable the message will reach him. I shall be hived up here three or four days longer without books or society—but to do the place justice I have seen a great deal worthy of observation.

Several persons belong'g to Canada have passed & I have gleaned something from all.

The emigration from England, Scotland & Germany to that Province is great. The disbanded soldiers take up a great deal of land—one hundred acres given as a bounty & they can't dispossess themselves. Three years rations are allowed from the Crown. This generous treatment one might reasonably presume would render them loyal subjects at the expiration of three years if the settlers have cleared a certain number of acres, built a frame barn & reside on the land it is then granted them in fee [simple]. Many of these soldiers I am told bid fair to make wholesome settlers. How they manage for wives nobody seems to know. Officers of rank & wealth have taken up their abode at Kin[g]ston & many people of wealth are among the late emigrants—from the U.S. no one goes now. They require something more than an oath of allegiances from the States since the war—attachment to a monarchial form of government & satisfactory proof that the stranger will make a loyal subject. Otherwise he is not admitted to purchace lands. These regulations together with the bitter animosity which the lower class of our countrymen particularly in this quarter feel toward Englishmen & the fear of a cold climate must eliminate all removals. The people of that country then must know less of ours & having no friends here can have no attachments. Should the Government of England hold out the same parental aid for years their hearts must be truly English & they a powerful people—but whether this is the case or not their interests will never lead them to join our confederation.

As things are situated now it is impossible for us with our whole disposable force to conquer that country.

Kingston itself is considered a second Quebec. $500,000 is said to have been expended in fortifying that place alone & so weak was it during the war that when Chauncey[47] appeared off the Town it had determined to surrender at summons but he was ignorant of this.

The laws of Province differ but slightly from those of the Mother Country—There is one peculiar to them which an Episcopalian Priest (his name M. Cartel) described grievous—no one can be married without a licence from the police & this licence is granted or not at their mere ipse dixit on the first application or not—sometimes a poor throbbing lover after riding more than one hundred miles for this privilege is kept in waiting or refused without rhyme or reason.

An Episcopalian parson however can marry or obtain a certificate for any one without delay. Their privileges are greater than those of other sects. All are countenanced except the Methodists

---

47. Isaac Chauncey (1772-1840) commanded the American naval forces on Lake Ontario during the War of 1812.

the priests of which sect are liable to imprisonment & every indignity. The church Priest in the true character of a Priest but not of a true Christian relished this from his heart. He told me that those societies (Episcopal) who were able to give a regular salary of 700 Dr. to their ministers received $800 from the Crown but an old Quaker whose word goes as far with me as the Priests denied the statement. There are one or two instances when the Crown allows this sum but it is arbitrary merely & not a systematic plan by any means.

The Quakers during the War obliged to pay a commutation tax to the amount of $40—in peace times it had been 20 Dr.

The distance across the lake [Ontario] from Sackets harbor to Kingston is forty miles. The Packet boats pass & repass every day. A Steam boat is building at the harbor to run to Niagara when that is in operation the Black river route will be the route to the Western Country in the Summer Season.

Sacket's Harbor will soon rival Ogdenburg. This the thirteenth of Sept.—rainy weather. A hard frost after this. I have hugged the fire all the week.

14th

The rain continuing—fire necessary—gloomy. Inquired of Grant the Taverner for books but the bible & psalm composed his stock & my hands were too unhallowed for their touch. Next applied to Capt. Schuyler who was equally literacy. Then to Mrs. Post[48] a very active smart woman. She had magazines she said but they proved

---

48. Mrs. John L. Post's husband was Francis's partner in developing a road through the tract (see p. 49). Their daughter Sophie kept house for Charles Herreshoff and wrote a letter from the tract to his family in Bristol, R.I., describing the last day (Dec. 19, 1819) of his life. In 1867 she wrote again to say that the graveyard in Boonville where he was buried was being taken by the railroad. She arranged for his remains to be exhumed and sent to Rhode Island, where they were interred in the North Burial Ground, Providence.

to be Evangelical. I trust my taste will never lead me to meddle with abstruse points in religion. My conduct will certainly not be less consonant to the pure & benevolent spirit of Christianity from this cause nor shall I in death be less resigned to the will of my creator— "his can't be wrong whose life is in the right".

In the awful moment all I can hope for is calmness & magnanimity and nature seldom denies them to a virtuous man.

Lead us not into temptation—

No person has suffered more from religious intolerance who so invariably perceived the happiness of man-kind vitally connected whith Christianism. A casual expression should never be taken for a fixed & serious opinion without subsequent & considerable corroboration. To say that I have much faith in the miracles & mysteries of religion is what I do not mean but that the system is an excellent one whether of divine or human origin is enough for me & whenever my expressions are construed otherwise injustice is done.

'Tis but too true however that the disregard of the ordinary forms of worship tho't so important in the land where some of the puritanism of our forefathers, left even in the minds of the most liberal & enlightened & now & then from "the heat of declamation" a mere spirit of perversity or the disgust which an exclusive hypocritical conduct inspires. The discovery of your contempt is taken advantage of & the ridicule which is only proper toward zealots is set down as an arrogant doubt or a positive denial of the whole system.

I am confirmed in the idea that to wound the religious feelings & prejudices of human beings is one of the worst species of cruelty. I would not disturb the simple Indian in his homage to the diety. It is enough that a man is happy in his creed & it answers the great purpose of making him a good citizen—any attempt of conversion from such a state is barbarous.

In this light I view all the missions to India. I entirely accord with Mr. [Thomas] Jefferson in the belief that it is of no consequence whether our neighbour worships one God or twenty Gods.

It neither picks our pockets or breaks our legs.

Is he an honest man! for an honest man's the noblest work of God—

This is all we have a right to enquire into—"Religious controversy is the offspring of arrogance & folly.

True piety is most laudably expressed by silence & submission.

Man ignorant of his own nature should not presume to scrutinize the nature of his God—it is sufficient for us to know that power & benevolence are the perfect attributes of the Deity" so says Gibbon[49] & he's a sound divine.

15th Sunday

The month of Sept. half gone & no answers to any of my letters. I am fearful some accident must have happened to my mother. She could not otherwise be so negligent to an only son. Moses [Brown Ives] too should have written. It is impossible my letters to him can have miscarried & equally so in either of these cases that the old adage will apply "out of sight out of mind". & therefore I'll wait patiently. When a man suspects his mother tis time for him to give over life. My case is not yet, thank God so deplorable. It is only to be hoped that I may never justly fall under suspicion.

Had my mare bro't out today & took Grant with me to the river. Brum the pilot after leaving the horses found the upper route decidedly inferior to the one I had marked the day before yesterday. I think I shall take that tho' one of the men thro' whose land we pass is murderously hostile—name Holhuen. The obstinacy & stupidity of these people about the direction of the road from the river surpassing all understanding if any degree of ignorance can be said to be unaccountable.

---

49. English historian Edward Gibbon (1737-1794), author of *The History of the Decline and Fall of the Roman Empire*, became a skeptic and a noted critic of Christianity after converting from Protestantism to Catholicism and back again.

Cap't Schuyler gave me a friendly visit this eve'g, a very clever man. Close to his own interest but contracted as traders & merchants generally are but mild & destitute of every particle of the malus animus.[50]

He describes Col. Mappa as the best liver in this western District. His house the abode of hospitality but he rarely goes abroad himself. The Capt. recommends his daughter for a wife!! The only objection he thought of was her want of beauty!!! was this all I could have? She must be most revoltingly ugly to affect me very disagreeably not that personal appearance has not its natural influence over me but the possession of beauty is no consideration in a wife—on the contrary as pretty women are generally vain & fond of admiration they are far [from] desirable. We do not expect a Venus de Medici. Mr. R says its impossible to define love—nature has so constituted us that no tastes correspond. The woman that might enchain my whole soul must of course give birth to something more than platonic affection. What I mean is it is not necessary nor even desirable that she should possess what the world calls beauty.

This has been my creed, from the moment I tho't of these matters the older I grow the more confirmed [am I] in the idea.

There is no meeting-house in this Town. In Turin a church is to be built McVickar & Constable[51] subscribe liberally & they expect aid from NYK. Live six or eight miles from this, C. just returned

---

50. "Malus animus": evil spirit.

51. William Constable, Jr., was the son of William Constable, who with Alexander Macomb and Daniel McCormick purchased over four million acres in upstate New York in 1791. Constable Sr. persuaded Paul Chassanis and Jacques LeRay (see n. 34, Part I and n. 12, Part III) to invest in the North Country. At his death in 1803, his son inherited a vast tract of raw land and built an estate, Constable Hall, in Constableville, just north of Boonville. Two years later he was killed in an accident. His widow, Mary Eliza McVickers Constable (sister of the McVickers mentioned above) lived on the estate another 50 years. Constable Hall is on the National Register of Historic Places and is now a museum.

[from] Ireland. Saw a couple of most beautiful greyhounds that he bro't with him.

16th

Cloudy dismal weather & Smith don't appear damn his blood but I have just discovered that the wind has changed from SE to the North. This should bring a clear day for according to the Bible "fair weather cometh from the north". They might have added with less risk in some countries or in the country where that was written but the truth of a proposition like this cannot affect the whole character of the book.—

I have been disturbed by the hypo. at intervals for a day or two back & lest the state of my mind at this moment should not be remember'd on my return to the banks of Warwick—let me acknowledge myself too little of a philosopher or too much disgusted with plebeian vulgarity & with many of the pursuits that might here be essential even from Choice to prefer this country even should matters wear a sombre aspect on my return I had rather encounter the deprivations which are accesible at S[pring] G[reen] even if fortune does her worst. But I have hopes—hopes of such a nature that I hardly dare avow them to myself.

I will not long remain in this state of doubt. As soon as I can get home I will & then see whether the plan that occupies the chief place in my heart is altogether illusory.

Tuesday 17th

The weather became charming yesterday tho' agreably to prophecy a severe frost visited us last night. Sent a letter to M[oses] B[rown] I[ves] Esq. this morn'g & then with a W. Hoyt explored the country again between this & our bridge place. He interest[ed] in the south route. This is fourth or fifth time I have been piloted thro'.

There is no reliance whatever to be placed on the information that is given. Tho' one man seemed to think that his neighbor could be depended on because he was a church member, but his neighbors interest he might have said coincided with his own. Interest is at the bottom of all things.

L'amour propre est le mobile de tout—

This obliges me to obtain a perfect knowledge of the geography of the country myself.

The man must have given me a chase to day of six miles—rejoiced to find Dibble & Ives at work on the river raising a chanty & preparing for the bridge. God speed them.

The day cannot be better. They commenced their operations yesterday. Ives bro't a boat down the river 12 miles as he judged.

18th

Another delightful day & no surveyor yet. The mail comes too & no letter to complete my misery I am out of employment having no books except the extract book & a vol of Shakespeare. The first only serves to raise recollections which it is painful to lull—to inspire courage & at the same moment to overwhelm with doubt & suspicion. The second has not the same ramifications. The book itself is connected with nothing important in my individual relations & stands therefore on its own bottom but who in the course of twenty five days would not become weary of one little vol—even the bible itself. Of the first book however in looking over it this morn'g I was struck with a theory from Allison[52] which as it seems to describe some of my feelings on the subject which Capt. Schuyler's advice gave birth to which I transcribe.

But it is chiefly in the beauty of the human countenance & form that the great purpose of nature is most apparent. When we feel these, it is not merely an <u>organic</u> or <u>animal</u> effect we experience. Whatever is lovely or beloved in the character of <u>mind</u> whatever in the powers or dispositions of man can awaken admiration or excite

---

52. Francis Allison (d. 1777), a distinguished minister and teacher, emigrated from Ireland to America in 1755 and settled in Philadelphia.

sensibility: the loveliness of innocence, the charms of opening genius, the varied tenderness of domestic affection, the dignity of heroic or the majesty of patriotic virtue; all these are expressed to us in the features of the countenance, or in the positions & movements of the form. While we behold them, we feel not only a feeling of temporary pleasure but what Lord Kaimes[53] had profoundly & emphatically called "the Sympathetic emotion of virtue" we shall in some measure in those high disposition[s], the expressions of which we contemplate our own bosoms glow with kindred sensibilities & we often return to life & to its virtues with minds either softened to a wider benevolence or awakened to a higher tone of morality. "Sympathy of taste is a pleasing attraction but congeniality of principle is the cement of souls."

This sentiment too in the same book awakened a long train of thought.

The interest excited by the quotations from Allison, Dupaty[54] Madame de Stail[55] and abstractedly without considering the selectionist only strengthened the idea which gave me in the onset the swing & impulse viz. that there was sympathy of taste: let there be only then congeniality of principle & according to the Partys own declaration succeeds the cement of souls.

The only question is how the wonder working congeniality

---

53. Henry Home, Lord Kames (1696-1782), was a senator in the College of Justice in Scotland and a well-known critic and philosopher. His principal works include *Sketches of the History of Man, Elements of Criticism,* and *The Gentleman Farmer.*

54. Dupaty (d. 1788) was president of the parliament of Bordeaux, an enlightened and eloquent French magistrate and writer.

55. Mme. Germaine de Staël (1766-1817), the French-Swiss novelist and critic, daughter of financier Jacques Necker, was a progressive in both public and private life. A republican and advocate of free love, her opposition to Napoleon's regime resulted in her banishment. She maintained brilliant salons in Paris and in exile near Geneva. Coincidentally, she and her father also invested in land in northern New York, through their friend Jacques LeRay (see n. 12, Part III).

should be brought to pass. But it is worse than idle in me to indulge such fantasies.

I went this afternoon with three men interested in different routes to measure two. The distance by the southern route to the east road one mile 37 chains & two miles forty five chains to the river. The man struck by no means a straight course by my compass. His object to get good ground—our way up on the line between 4 & 5 one mile & two chains. The chainmen at loggerheads all the way—Sat without a fire for the first time this eve'g since my return from Lowville.

Thursday 19th Sept
Brum came to my door to say that he had measured from the east road to the State road at Rogers house & found the distance one mile & twenty seven chains. This route to the river therefore 1/4 of a mile less than the one we measured down.

The day as pleasant as yesterday. Put on thin pantaloons again. From some cause or other could not sleep last night—never recollect to have been so restless when in health. It was Black River or Providence river—a struggle between a life of activity & enterprise with influence & its concomitant cares & a life in a smaller spere of action the world forgetting by the world forgot. But however the first might preponderate as a simple case of itself yet the impossibility of removing myself from my mother is always the stumbling block. With this & one other <u>chose</u> hors du combat B[lack] River has the decided preference. But if this other chose proves something more than moonshine then all for—& the world well lost—

> All the world's a stage
> And all the men & women merely players
> They have their exits & their entrances;
> And one man in his time plays many parts,
> His acts bring seven ages. At first the infant
> Mewling & puking in his nurse's arms:

And then the whining schoolboy with his satchel
And shining morn'g face, creeping like a snail
Unwillingly to school: And then the lover,
Sighing like furnaces with a woeful ballad
Made to his mistress' eye brow. Then a Soldier
Full of strange oaths & bearded like the bard,
Zealous in honor sudden & quick in quarrel,
Seeking the bubble reputation
Even in the common's mouth: & then, the justice,
In fair round belly, with good capon lin'd
with eyes severs, & beard of formal cut
Fullof wise saws & modern instances
And so he plays his part: The sixth age shifts
Into the lean & slipper'd pantaloon:
With spectacles on nose, & pouch on side:
His youthful hose well saved, a world too wide
For his shrunk shank; & his big manly voice,
Turning again to childish treble pipes
And whistles in his sound: Last scene of all,
That ends this strange eventful history
Is second childishness & mere oblivion
Sans teeth, sans eyes, sans taste, sans everything.[56]

Bucked up for the first time since I left Utica & felt more like a Christian. Then called on Col. Mappa. This gentleman about 60 years of age emigrated from Holland before the year 90 in a vessel belon'g to Newport [merchant] Mr. Gibbs[57]—[Mappa] a man of education who has seen a great deal of the world very courteous in his manners & a pleasant companion—his daughter instead of

---

56. *As You Like It,* Act II, Scene 7.

57. George Gibbs (1735-1803), one of Newport's great merchants, traded extensively with the West Indies before the Revolution. After the war he and his brother-in-law Walter Channing amassed a fleet of 75 ships that traded worldwide.

being eighteen must be nearer two score—so much for Capt. Schuyler. Her head set on her shoulders in the true Dutch Flanders mare style. It was agreable however to see a woman again who had the manners even of a Lady. In this respect she is by no means deficient. She said but little & I as usual was dumb foundered. She has the appearance of a studious character.

Her Father very desirous to obtain my opinions of the value of the part of this Tract I traversed with the Surveyor the other day. Offer'd it me at three dollars [per acre]. That is to say in an indirect way. He has seen many people who have returned disgusted with the Ohio country. The land dearer there than here & the market inferior. This is an argument that balances the advantage of climate—if the soil yields as abundantly here or half as much so the crop is worth more—but it is not contended that for grazing we are not a match. There will be a time of tide yet in our affairs which may lead to greatness.

The Col. with all his experiences & all his caution think there can be no better speculation under present discouragement even, than the purchase of one of these Tracts. For instance the east Adgate [Tract] 12000 acres for immediate settlement but not unless the Proprietor settles himself on the premises. In this case he seemed to imply that almost any accessible inhabitable place would gradually [attract] people.

This argument would have weighted more with me when I knew less of my own tastes. A very little persuasion would have turned the scales with me last season—but now—

This Tract has been taxed since the year 93. The Col. has never sold over 10 Dr tho' many of the lots have been resold at 15 Dr—wild land.

They sold at first for 1-1/2 Dr but this he thinks the great error. The cause of bringing a shiftless idle race of settlers whose bad husbandry & bad character gave the country an unpromising reputation & stopped or diverted the channel of emigration. Another evil they have had to encounter is the making of roads at their own expense & then having to pay for others which were of no service. The division of the Tract into separate Townships is still another evil... Taxes, Taxes this is the head & front of all deviltry.

20th
The morn'g pleasant & the Surveyor not arrived—but clouds soon thicken around & the equinoctial [storm] may be expected. A long & tedious storm & all our operations suspended. The last week as delightful weather as the heart could wish has thus been irretrievably lost by the non performance of Smith's engagement but it is useless to quarrel with him. Tho' it would do me good to go thro' St [?] ruined plus curse.

Saturday 21st Sept.
Glory be to God in the highest on Earth peace & Smith is at length arrived & the day contrary to all expectation proved delightful. A heavy frost last night having settled the weather.

Scrawled a line this morn'g to my mother & dispatched Smith with three hands to find two routes to the river intending on his return to cross & proceed towards the majestic banks of Moose River.

Called on Mrs. Post—not at home. The good woman had left some chocolate hearing my distress for that article. Bo't Pork at 18 cents the lb!! & whiskey at a dollar the gallon from Southwell, bread of Grant, onions & a little tea also, maple sugar always miserable stuff of Schuyler.

I did not pass the office & I am still in the dark. If the prayers of the wicked availed mine should be raised for the choice spirits of Providence.

I have been very much pleased with Col. Mappa—with Mrs. Grant the Taverner's wife also a very pretty as well as tolerably smart woman. They have a chunky welch maid & an Austrian ost-[l]er a civil fellow who knows his place. They have all been very attentive to me.

Sunday Sept. 22nd

Leave the village road a little more than half a mile from Grants & [struck] the east road at Fisks. Then to the river thro' the clearings of Dodge Hoyt & Thayer to the river accompanied by chainmen, the Surveyor a marksman & a dozen volunteers.

20lb of hard bread besides one loaf of soft

15lb Pork

3lb Sugar

1lb chocolate

1/2lb Tea

raw onions, fire works, axe, 3 qts whiskey & blankets compose our packs.

At the river found an assemblage of men, women & children drawn together from the fame of our bridge. We crossed in a boat. Ives & Dibble hard at work building pier which looks well as I could wish. There were several young lasses bedecked in their Sunday clothes & surrounded by lovers. They were not driven from their embracements by our approach. The girls sat in the laps of their swain, on the wilderness side of the roaring flood in the true style of romance until I called them to bring us over. Perhaps they had better be at meeting but this is questi vescata [?]. My only complaint is the publicity of courtship.

But a familiarity which with us would be allowable only after the fatal yes is perfectly accordant with their ideas of propriety. The ardency of the gallant is not restrained from any fears whatsoever. The consequences are prehaps sometimes unfortunate. As "rebellious nature will assert her rights". These matters however will be regulated by the degree of refinement at which Society has arrived. What criteria of virtue is not to be ascertained for in the Spartan age of N[ew] E[ngland] the practice of bundling prevailed. I am writing now by an awful fire seated on hemlock bows. We have determined to sleep without a covering. The weather being fine & the bark refusing to peal. Our course has been good.

Sept. 23rd

One year this day since the memorable storm on the sea board.[58]
God preserve them from such another. A clear day. We slept in
great comfort tho' two of our men were indisposed.

The remedy applied to one was novel to me. His complaint a
violent pain in the back—for this he was laid on his belly & one of
the men danced on his back!! It is not less singular that he found
relief from the barbarous prescription.

I am now at the extremity of a plain on which we have travelled
all the morn'g without finding water.

The men at present in the rear & following the sound of my
voice. I hear a stream at the foot of the hill where I sit. We must
dive there [when] the button denotes the hour of two—what a
strange phenomenon!!

I am a little fearful of rain. It will be a death blow to our
business if it should. Land covered principally with hard timber—
excellent without exception after dinner. To straighten our course
or rather to get a good one thro' this gulph Smith has gone ahead of
me. I am at the banks of a stream large enough for a mill. Prindle is
back of me, Grant of him & Brum at the compass. Smith screaching
first & all of us in succession—a curious way of finding a route thro'
the wilderness. One of which I lay claim to the invention—for
Heaven knows as little ingenuity as there may be in it patents have
been obtained for less. For instance our cousin Jere's[59] punch bowl
boat. Smith returns & always has good luck or [so] he says.

---

58. The Great Gale of September 23, 1815, was a full-blown hurricane—a rare and
poorly understood phenomenon in New England at that time. A so-called equinoctial gale (see p. 41, line 6) coinciding with the autumn equinox, the 1815 storm
hit at high tide, flooding downtown Providence to a depth of six feet or more,
destroying the port's bridges, docks, warehouses, and ships, as well as the city's
commercial and market center. The Brown family enterprises at India Point,
including a distillery, were all lost.

59. Capt. Jeremiah Brown (1746-1817), son of Deputy Governor Elisha Brown.

24th Sept.

The rain made us uncomfortable but we regained our old chanty near Moose river. The earth was on fire for a considerable distance around. We had made this fire the last day of August. It had not however consumed the back of our chanty which was infinitely valuable to us in a rain when the trees would no longer peal. The pumkies bite so damnable that I can sit in no comfort—chanty on the banks of Moose river. The day occupied principally in searching routes. The weather being fine conclude to take no trouble about a covering. I went to the river alone & having determined on a bridge place the men run the line to my voice.

The river not so broad here as at our crossing place on B River. That measured 3 chains 50 links or 13 rods. Now on my Township against my inclination but there is no help.

Brum has set fire to an old dead tree which burns most majestically. The blaze reaching 80 or one hundred feet & the whole surrounding wilderness illuminated. We have fears for our chanty but fear will hardly keep our eyes open. There is nothing like fatigue.

25th Sept.

Go back with the whole party to rectify the course. Agree with Prindle to cut a road out between the rivers for 12-1/2 Dollars the mile—one rod width to be done immediately. Then dismiss him. Brum & Grant who expect to reach B. River to night then with I return to M[oose] R[iver] where I now am examing bridge places & routes etc.

M.R. an excellent place for a saw mill.

26th Sept.

This night on the banks of the river, fire raging on all sides. Obliged to desert the chanty!! Saw mill, being only 8 or 9 miles. Good land conveyance to the settled country. Homes may be made in many places hereabouts & water enough obtained to carry all the cotton spindles in R.I. Spruce timber of first quality. Price one dollar the hundred, clear stuff, 5/ Hemlock.

27 Sept.

The night a very severe one & having no axe were unable to pro-
cure wood enough to make us comfortable. Occupied one of Gay's
camps—a miserable place. The fire had burned the ground two or
three feet lower than the chanty—it was literally in a cellar & I
spent some hours of the night <u>anathematisating</u> & not in prayer of
thanksgiving.

But after the most severe trial of this campaign I have to thank
God for the preservation of my health when the noon fatigue
overpower'd hard frames—& for my safe return to the Settlement.
Nothing remarkable happened this last days cruise <u>saving</u> & except
our having incountered a hedge hog whom we left a lifeless corpse.
Saw two Deer on our route. Walked in Joys road nine miles examing it & dissatisfied.

∾∾∾

Notes in back of diary:

Course from B.R. on the line of Lots 4 & 5
>   40 all level as a house floor after riding the short pitch at
>   the river.
>   then leave the line & go to the left
>   22 to mill creek one chain across—
>   2 to a large maple stand'g in an old path
>   2 to the east road

Course from State road towards B River about E.N.E.
>   30 chains to Cummings Creek
>   10 chains to a birch tree
>   10 & have the village road course N.E.
>   cr'se a short pitch 30 not level nor had land dry but parallel
>   with old road.
>   17   50 links to a brook runn'g west

wst 2 rods
19   50 to the east road
3
20 descending not bad
7 to Hoyt cleari'g
13 tolerably good
34 to Brums line
6 down a precipice & then flat to the river
5 chains—
Brown Tract poor land all the lots from 331 to 336—from 345 to 348—from 354 to 358 & 364 & 365.
73 Lotts or 14,600 acres first rate or excellent land
186 Lotts—37,200 second best or good land
112 Lotts—22,400 poor land
72,200 acres of which 57,800 are saleable and 22,400. acres poor

Memo written in front of diary:

Agreed with the two Dodges to make a road from the Boonville village road to Black River for 30 Dr the mile—to be cut smoothed & cleared out one rod in width before winter sets in & to be slashed one rod each side of this rod during the winter.

1816—9th Octo—part of agreement —
    Crooks to be gradual & the starting place the third blazed hemlock on the left going from Grants.—

Notes in flyleaf of diary listing towns, villages, mileage, inns and innkeepers between Albany and Providence:

Greenbush
Schodack—5 miles
Nassau—16 miles from Albany—Bainard [innkeeper]
New Lebanon—Hull [innkeeper] Hancocck
Cohen   Pittsfield   Morgan
Dalton—Waterman

Peru

Dunn's——Worthington Corners

Chesterfields—Parsons

Northampton—Edwards   Chapman

Hadley

Belchertown—Claps

Ware

Western

Brookfield—Rices

Sturbridge

Charlton

Oxford—Campbells

Sutton

Douglas

Burrillville—Walden

Smithfield—D. Angell

North Providence

Providence

Notes on land taxes in the Adirondacks:

Road from Turin to Emilyville.

Watson's TAX

North Triangle	$	642.86
South D...........		950.72
	$1,593.58	

Herreshoffs TAX

No. 3..................		$55.41
No. 5................		19.26
	$74.67	

J.B. Francis TAX

on No. 4..........	$637.66

TAX paid at the Office of the Treasurer of NYK as certified by the comptroller in Albany Saturday August 10th 1816.

Appendix to Part I: Roads on the Brown Tract

In May of 1799 John Brown, grandfather of John Brown Francis, began construction of a road from Remsen to Settlement No. 1 (which he named Sobriety), terminating "near the south shore of the Middle Branch of the Moose River" close to the present-day town of Old Forge. By 1811 the road was in disrepair, as John Brown Francis reported after inspecting it in company with his uncle, Charles Herreshoff. He wrote that the bridge over the Black River "constructed by my grandfather is weak & tottering, too much so for use. The road from here was also made by him; it was never good & it is inexecessable, large trees have blown over, bushes & brambles have grown up, causeways gone to decay, & bridges swept off or broken down. The path crooked & the branches of the lofty trees obstruct the rays of the sun. We were often obliged to dismount & lead our horses round the prostrate trees or compel them to jump over."

Francis goes on to state that "a good road must be made," and in 1815 he petitioned the New York legislature to permit construction of a new road using state funds rather than his own. As the following Act (reproduced here exactly as Francis transcribed it in the diary) indicates, Francis and his fellow commissioners, Stephen Smith and John L. Post, would be responsible for surveying, clearing and constructing the road, and assessing taxes on the land through which it passed. Work began in August 1816, as described in Part I of the diary. The new road was laid out from Boonville to Settlement No. 1, passing through Thendara (the site of Charles Herreshoff's "mansion") to Old Forge, completely abandoning the old Remsen road built by John Brown.

An act for opening & improving a road from Boonville to the road leading from the City of Albany to the St. Lawrence passed April 15, 1816.

Preamble:

Whereas Thomas Logan, John Brown Francis and others, owners of land through which the road herein after mentioned is to pass & which will be affected thereby, have by their petition represented to the Legislature, that a road being opened from the northerly part of Boonville, running Southeasterly until it intersect the road from the city of Albany to the river St. Lawrence, would be useful to the public & beneficial to the owners of the land through which the same should pass & have prayed that an act may be passed for the purposes & with provisions herein after contained; Therefore Commissioners Be it enacted by the People of the State of New York represented in Senate & Assembly. That John Brown Francis, Stephen Smith 2nd and John L. Post be & they are hereby appointed commissioners for exploring & marking out a route for a road, from the northerly part of the town of Boonville to intersect the road leading from the City of Albany to the St. Lawrence, in or near Township no. 41 of Totten & Crossfields Purchase, in such place as they shall judge most eligible & advantageous for a road.

Money to be raised for making the road.

II And be it further enacted, That there shall be assessed paid & collected for the purpose of opening & making said road, viz: on every acre of land, lying within one mile of said road a sum not exceeding six cents nor less than three cents & on every acre of land lying within two miles of said road & more than one mile, a sum not exceeding three cents, nor less than one cent except the lands belonging to the People of this the assessment to be proportioned to the value of the land so assessed.

III Duty of the Commissioners And be it further enacted That the commissioners shall have power to open & make the said road in such direction as they shall think most advisable for the public good: & also to make the assessment on the lands herein made subject to this tax as aforsaid: And said Commissioners are hereby required, as soon as may be after the route for the said road shall be fixed upon & marked by them, to, ASSESSMENTS, make and examine a fair assessment on the lands herein made subject to this tax as aforesaid: which assessment shall be in writing

& shall ascertain & describe the parcels of land so assessed, as accurately as may be; & the same shall be filed in the Comptroller's office, whose duty it shall be to give notice in some newspaper printed in the city of New York & also in one newspaper printed in the city of Albany for three successive weeks, that he has received on assessment of a tax made agreeably to this act; & that unless the said tax shall be paid within six LANDS may be sold
months after the date of said advertisement, it shall then be the duty of the comptroller to sell all the Lands on which the tax aforesaid shall remain unpaid, or so much of the same as may be necessary to raise the amount of the sum so assessed & remaining unpaid, together with all the expenses that shall have arisen on the same, in the same way & manner; & at the next succeeding sale he shall make under the law for the assessment & collection of taxes, and have the same authority to convey the same lands so sold & to receive the same interest & allow the same length of time for the redemption of the same, as he is authorized to do under the several laws regulating the sale of land for taxes; & it shall be the duty of the Treasurer to pay over said money to the Commissioner appointed by this act, on the warrant of the comptroller, that act, that the said tax so returned shall amount to, at the examination of six months above mentioned if wanted for the purpose of making the road authorized to be opened & improved by this act: & the comptroller shall require the said commissioners to account for the same according to Law.

IV Bonds to be given
And be it further enacted that each of the commissioners appointed under this act shall give bonds with surety to be approved by the comptroller of this State, for the sum of five thousand dollars, with condition, faithfully to perform all things required of them by this act according to the true intent & meaning thereof, which bonds shall be deposited in the comptroller's office before they shall receive any of the aforesaid money.

Expenses of making the road Thro' state Land to be paid
And be it further enacted That where the said road shall pass through Land belonging to the People of this State, it shall be the duty of the Commissioners to keep a distinct account of the expenses incurred in opening & improving such part of said road, & upon presenting such account, duly authenticated, to the comptroller, it shall be the duty of the

Comptroller to draw his warrant on the treasurer, in favor of said commissioners for the amount of the same, & the treasurer shall pay the same out of any monies in the treasury not otherwise appropriated, provided it does not exceed four hundred dollars.

Persons making the road Thro' their Lands not to be taxed

VI And be it further enacted that the owner or occupant of any land, thro' which the said road may pass & who shall actually make the said road at his own expense, thro' the said land, according to the directions of said Commissioners shall be discharged from any tax or assessment on the said lands, to which he would otherwise be liable.

Pay of the Commissioners

VII And be it further enacted That the commissioners appointed under this act, shall each of them be entitled to receive two dollars for each days service in which they shall be employed in exploring marking & laying out the said road, together with wages & necessary expenses of such persons as they shall necessarily employ to assist them in executing the same; & that the said commissioners shall be entitled to receive two & one half per cent on all monies which they shall expend for the purpose of opening & completing the road, as a compensation for making the assessments on the land, as well as contracting for & superintending the completion of said road.

Vacancies how to be filled

VIII And be it further enacted That in case of the death, refusal to act, or resignation of any person appointed by this act to be a commissioner it shall & may be lawful for the person administrating the government of this State, to supply va[ca]ncy by the appointment of such person to fill the same as he in his discretion shall deem meet or proper.

Two shall form a quorum

IX And be it further enacted that two of the commissioners hereby appoint[ed] shall be deemed a quorum who may transact all business incident to the [?] reposed in them by this act.

Chapter CLII   page 164   Session Laws 1816   39th Session.

PART II — 1817

Left Providence the 10th June.

Brown's Tract June 20, 1817 on Township No. 1 at the middle settlement on my way to Boonville.

I arrived in that place on Monday the 16th just one week from Providence having passed one day in Albany & two in Utica—The stage brought me the first day to Hartford a distance of 70 miles the second to Albany 96 miles & the third I rode in the afternoon to Schenectady. Saw Mr. Nott.[1] The next night lodged in Utica. The weather has been bad all the way—intolerably so between Albany & Utica. There was a frost throughout the cold region on the 15th & a very severe one which killed the potatoes & crops on the 16th.

On the Tract the loss [has] not been more severe. The English grain is backward but never looked more promising. The Potatoes just coming up. It has rained plentifully since my arrival on the Tract & almost every day or night in greater or less quantities since I left home.

My horse is now at large enjoying the fine feed of the old clearing. The day delightful & the mosquitoes not troublesome.

There is less calculation to be made on the weather in this mountain climate than in R.I. I rode the last two hours in a soaking rain & was exposed in addition to this misery, to the perils of falling trees. The wind raged & the crash of trees with the rolling thunder had quite enough of the grand & terrific in it.

On Sunday morn'g went to hear the Unitarian Parson from

---

1. Rev. Eliphalet Nott (1773-1866), a 1795 graduate of Rhode Island College, in 1804 was named president of Union College in Schenectady, one of the nation's oldest liberal-arts colleges. He held that post for 62 years until his death at age 93. Some of the landscaping of the campus was done by Elkanah Watson (see n. 13, Part I), who planted poplar trees to form a "grove of academe" around the college edifice.

Trenton. His name Pearce formerly of North Kingston, R.I. He is rather above the level of the ordinary gentleman of his Profession & handled his doctrine very ingeniously.

23rd June
Mr. H[erreshoff] arrives in the stage.

24th
Smith appears, engage him to work on the road with a gang of five or eight—to have 2 Doll's a day & be allowed three doll's a week for boarding the men.

25
Went with Smith to Leyden to buy wheat & pork. The prices of the first article 2 Ds. the bushel, Pork 23, Prime 30, mess Potatoes 50 cts.

Grant's horse a great traveller & come near breaking my neck.

26th
With Mr. H, two women, a hunter, & Nicholas Vincent, three pack horses & two cows—in all five souls & mine. Beasts proceeded to the Tract road beyond Moose River—horribly bad. 11 hours going 20 miles & half way in the rain.

27
All went well on the Tract—a fine day. Went to the n[orth] branch to be bit by mosquitoes for we caught no fish.

28
Gardener & Ives go out with Schuyler's horses. Call to see Hofford & family. Child three years old badly burnt last February—crippled for life I expect—Saw Mr. Vincent & settled with Major Joy.

29th Sunday

Blustering weather. Set off on an expedition to the fourth Lake, prepared to pass the night out, but relinquished the undertaking at the mill. White having taken our boat. We could not have gone had it been there, the wind being too high & ahead with occasional showers.

Mr. H. remarked that the high winds were unknown here as far back as 1811.

Hafford the runaway returned last night—confirms the death of poor Captain Gould[2] by a kick in the testicles from an ox. The boys take care of Grammy by their Father's dying request.

30th

Fine weather. Go with Major Joy & Mr. H. to search a route for the road better than the present one to the westward of this clearing—one mile from [?] house. Supposed to be in Township No. 7 as far as the mile & half tree.

Land hereabouts excellent for pasture.

Mr. H.'s clearing on my land by mistake.

Mrs. Vincent had a tea party this afternoon. Six smart women, one only unmarried compose the party.

The road runs nearly a quarter of a mile thro' the clearing on lot No. 11. 2nd range which is the lot south of the land I exchanged & is all on land belonging to me in No. 7 about a mile.

---

2. Capt. James Gould, a Revolutionary War veteran who settled in the North Country, was hired by John Brown to construct hundreds of miles of roads through the Brown Tract at $10 per mile. In 1799 he purchased a 200-acre farm in Township No. 7, and by 1814 he had cleared enough land to plant a 70-tree apple orchard and fields of rye. Christine Jerome, in *An Adirondack Passage*, describes Captain Gould as one of the unluckiest settlers on the Brown Tract. Three years before his bizarre death, he had ridden off "in his best clothes...to claim the widow who had agreed to marry him"—only to discover that she had jilted him for a wealthier man.

1st July

Hug the fire—cold uncomfortable—rainy day.

Morgan the Hunter & White come down the lake—the water very high 12 miles from the mills. It has not settled three inches this season—this a remarkable case & unfortunate for Mr. H who is anxious to examine the beach for black sand.3

Another tea party this afternoon. All the women on the Tract present making of eight precious souls. Pound cake, preserved currants etc. for the entertainment!

2nd July

Fine cloudless day. George Grave from Russia comes to purchase Mr. H.'s wool,4 taked most of it on shares. He to have one half of the cloth. Mr. H. had previously sold common wool for 50 cts. & half, & three quarters blood for 75 cts.

Examine the road between the bridge & Joy's. The present route must be followed. An angle may be saved by passing the Major's meadow which he don't relish.

White goes off about 15 miles thro' the woods to lug back on his head a bark canoe.

Go to Crosby's clearing—the feed excellent.

3rd July

The air in the dog day style. Everything looks flourishing. The grass

---

3. Black sand indicated the presence of iron.

4. In 1812 Charles Herreshoff first broached the possibility of raising sheep on the Tract—an idea that John Brown Francis received with caution, reminding his uncle of the unknown disease that had decimated his flock in Bristol and warning, "We had better investigate the secret cause if possible & not plunge heedlessly into the unexplored oceans of experiments." Herreshoff went ahead anyway, constructing a 4,500-square-foot sheep barn in 1815, assembling a flock of 300 sheep in Providence, and having them driven overland to the Adirondacks—a trek that took six weeks. Within three years hostile weather, disease, and wolves reduced their numbers by more than half.

as well as the grain.

Vincent returns with four pack horses.

4th July

The same heat continues. All hands disposed to spend the day in frolick. Go with them to the mills where they play ball5 all day & I look on, exposed to a baking sun.

July 5th

With old Vincent & Major Joy set off for Boonville. Find Smith at Black River, he had commenced his operation this day. Chantied at the river last night.

Post comes over to see me & carries me to his house with his usual hospitality. Introduced to Mr. Constable6 one of the landed proprietors in this neighborhood. Has the manners of a man who has seen good company.

The pumpkies have annoyed me dreadfully these two days past.

Our thermometer was broken but the mercury must have been above eighty for three days in succession, between 85 & 90 today perhaps.

The price of potatoes hereabouts six shillings. Flour 12 Doll's—wages from 14 to 16 doll's.

Sunday July 6th

Hot weather with occasional showers. Dine with Mr. Post. Write Aunt F., John & Uncle C.7

---

5. Francis apparently refers to baseball, which would make this the first known record of the game being played in the Adirondack region.

6. See n. 53, part I.

7. Elizabeth Powel Francis, John Brown Francis's paternal aunt, married Joshua Fisher of Philadelphia in 1777. Charles Francis (1771-1845), also of Philadelphia, was his (unmarried) paternal uncle.

7th

Clear & pleasant. Find Smith at the mile brook with six hands hard at work. Commenced yesterday himself with one man & with the whole gang this morn'g.

8th

Warm & showery. Dined with Schuyler in company with a Mr. Alsop lately removed from the Jersey's to Turin & Judge McVickar of whom he has purchased largely.

Went to see the road & got wet.

I go to 4 mile creek tomorrow.

9th

Cool cloudless day. Joy goes with the first team thro' [?] road.

10th

With Mr. Post, Smith & Chris John go to Moose River to inspect the cradle knolls & dugways of Brum. Decided unanimously not to be done & Brum notified accordingly.

Then up the river to ascertain whether a bridge could have been made at a less expense where it was contemplated to build one at the time D[ibble] & I[ves] took their job & decided by Smith & myself <u>not</u>.

Smith is chantied at the 4 mile creek—

There are said to be three hundred [settlers] within the limits of Canandaigua![8] So much for the glorious uncertainty of trade.

Post almost beaten out by the exertion of the day. Mrs. P. near her confinement. Breakfasted & suppered with her ladyship.

---

8. The growth of Canandaigua, in the Finger Lakes district, began in 1789 when Gen. Israel Chapin of New England resettled there. Within a few years the town was flooded with settlers moving west. Like others who tried to develop Brown's Tract, John Brown Francis apparently chose to downplay the rich farming potential and longer growing season of the state's western regions.

11th

A rain prevents me from going to the Tract. A fire rekindled in the hearth & eating room.

Brum returns & says he has made fifty three rod of log way on the other side of Moose River. He swears that he will do nothing more to the hundred dollar job. Not one of the men who have taken jobs are satisfied with us or we with them. So impracticable it is to deal with the vagabones in this quarter without imposition.

12th Saturday

With five pounds of powder & seven of sugar in a good pair of saddle bags set off for the Tract—flattering weather.

The rain poured in torrents from the mile creek to Moose river a distance of nine miles!

Wet thro' & thro' & no whiskey or spirits of any sort.

Arrived & found Mr. H. blowing rocks for iron ore—1/2 past 4 o'clock. The rye on the Hill looks charmingly. The grass also— pretty well at the middle settlement.

13th

A fine day—walk on the hill to see the grain. The oats & rye of a monstrous growth. Wheat has not come up well, but is notwith- standing very strong & healthy. Potatoes backward but thrifty. The promise of a great crop from all these—buck wheat too.

14th

Clear cool a slight frost here, no mischief done, no symptoms of frost at Goulds.

Agree with White to take a tour up the lakes—Enos comes in, says Smith was building a chanty at the 2 mile log way (from Moose river) when he passed.

15th

Fair—very hot in the middle of the day. White bro't us a quarter of venison yesterday & a second today. It is always lean at this season but it was tender & palatable.

Wednesday 16th
Very warm again. Mr. H. thinks the mercury would rise to ninety.

Captain Prindle arrives & has almost pursuaded me to go out with him tomorrow.

Thursday 17
Oppressingly hot. Set out for Smith's camp with Prindle. Meet Joy on the road who gives me a letter from M[oses] B[rown] I[ves]. Had a little sparring with the Major & left him in very ill blood. He has cheated me out of 85 dollars in the most barefaced manner. I threatened him with prosecution for burning my barn—called him a cheat & left him.

Stopped 30 minutes with Smith in which time we come to terms with Prindle. Drank tea with Post.

18
Same kind of weather. Received a letter from Eliza. I had almost made up my mind for a trip to Niagara yesterday but circumstances seem not to admit of it.

Now I think of departing for Providence by the first stage.

Saturday 19th
Leave Boonville in the afternoon for Utica. Sultry air & dusty but slight shower at night. I have been entrusted with three packages of money for Albany this afternoon, one from an entire stranger.

20
Leave Utica at 1/2 past two, a fine cool day. Road excessively rough, arrive in Albany about nine. So dusty we could scarcely breathe for the last twenty miles.

21

Pass this day in Albany at the mansion house north Market street. Kept by one Skinner—excellent house.9

Called on the [Elkanah] Watsons. Mrs. W. as clever as ever. The daughter a conceited little thing. Their son George to be married at Pittsfield, lives in fine house.

22nd

A cold rain—breakfast at Green River miserable house, dine in Norfolk 35 miles from N Sheffield a very pleasant town, a good tavern kept there by one Ensign.10 Crops thro' this country excellent.

Left at 2 & arrived in H[artford] at 9.

The first part of the way suffered from cold then from wet. The stage being crakey.11 Cleared off delightful.

23 July

Leave Hartford at six, breakfast at Pomroys in Coventry12 16 miles.

Porters in Hartford pretty good house.

Arrive in Providence before sun set. Family out of Town—all well.

29th July
1817

ᘉᘉᘉ

---

9. E.W. Skinner owned the Mansion House at 349 North Market Street, Albany.

10. Ensign's tavern on the Green was built by Giles Pettibone, Jr. in 1794.

11. "Crankey" is an old sea term that came ashore, originally describing a merchant vessel that lacked enough ballast to make it stable. In the stagecoach era it was adapted to mean a lightly loaded, unbalanced vehicle.

12. Eleazer Pomeroy's Tavern on the old Boston Turnpike was built ca. 1801-04; it still stands and is now a private home.

Notes on flyleaf of diary, Part II:

Memo: To buy at Albany Gov. Clinton's address an essay before the anti-slavery society—also the report of the Society [to] prevent pauperism.

Purchased a Thermometer and a coffee mill at Utica.

Jas. Benton; Mr. H. fireman

Chopping 6 Dr. the acre—clearing from 13 to 15

Gave the Major Joy an order on Mr. Post for 179 Dr. 37 cts being the bal. due him for the road cut thro' No. 1
Whole cost of his work $679.37-1/2
George R. Vincent $16
Chauncy Vincent $16
William Perry 16

1817
on acct. of the road

June	18	pd Joy on the Tract $100	
"	23	Brum	5
"	25	Smith at Boonville	
"	26	Ditto—	100
"	28	Abiathai Joy on Brown Tract	
			120

Bridge over the Moose River

Chris John	10 days	$10
Dibble & Ives	11 days	22.
Charles Viner	11 "/50 cts	6.50
Brum	8 "	8.00
Mr. Jones	8-1/2" 6.50	
Caroler Churchill with oxen	7 .50	10.50
Sam Rowland & oxen	11 8/	11.
	67 days	$74.50

Board

Say 10 weeks	13 Dr. 30
Liquor	15
Fodder	5.75
" from BT	3.25
BT Team	5.25
BT work	23.
D. & I. first	27.50
	$184.25

C.F.H. on Estate acc't bal:
  due the 1st April 1817 $2785.43

26 June 1817
Memo
Agreed with Steven Smith to come out on the road as soon as may
be with five hands or more to board them at 3 Doll. a week & have
the superintendance of them in improving the road from B[lack]
River to the settlement—they to be hired by the day at two Dolls.
exclusive of board—he to sell his oxen to the road for $5 Dolls.—
tools to be furnished by the road.

1. Portrait miniature of John Brown by Edward Greene Malbone.
(Courtesy New-York Historical Society.)

2. John Francis, father of John Brown Francis. Silhouette by Miers of London. (Courtesy Rhode Island Historical Society.)

3. Abby Brown Francis, mother of John Brown Francis. (Courtesy of Mrs. Maurice Washburne.)

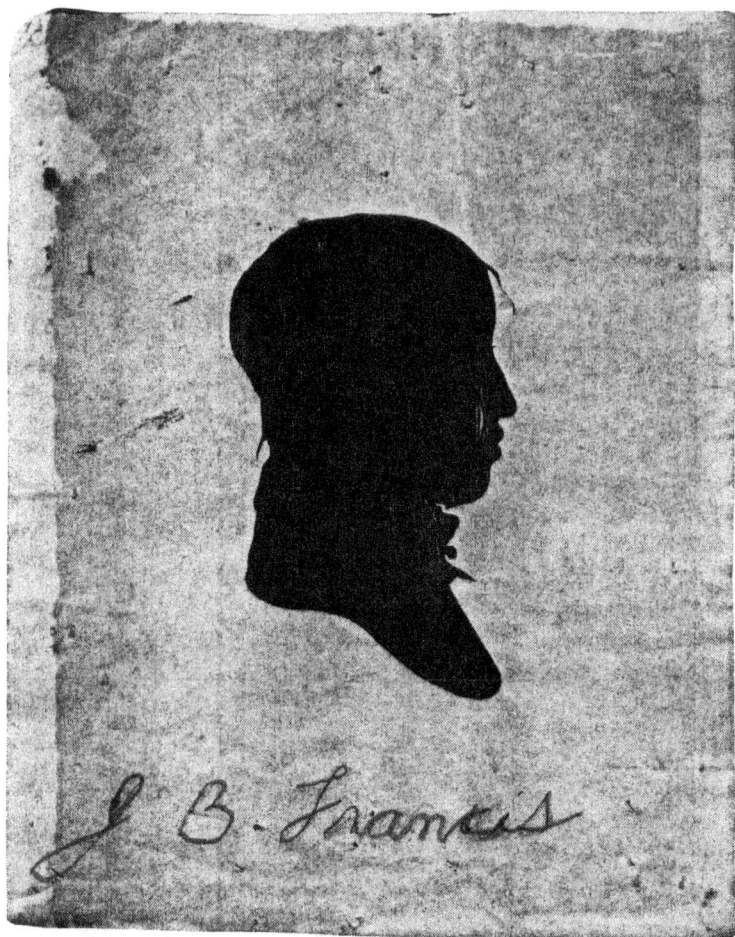

4. Silhouette of John Brown Francis (age 11-12) by Baché of Philadelphia, circa 1803.

5. The Greene house (built ca. 1690), Spring Green Farm, Warwick, R.I.

6. Daniel Angell tavern, Smithfield, R.I. Now a private home.

7. Walden's Tavern (now the Western Hotel), Burrillville, R.I.

8. The Rice homestead, Brookfield, Mass.

9. State Capitol, Albany, N.Y., 1811. Lithograph by Pendleton after a drawing by Henry Walton. (Courtesy New-York Historical Society.)

10. Francis received this painted silk "Friendship presents" token from Eliza (Wister?), ca. 1815-16.

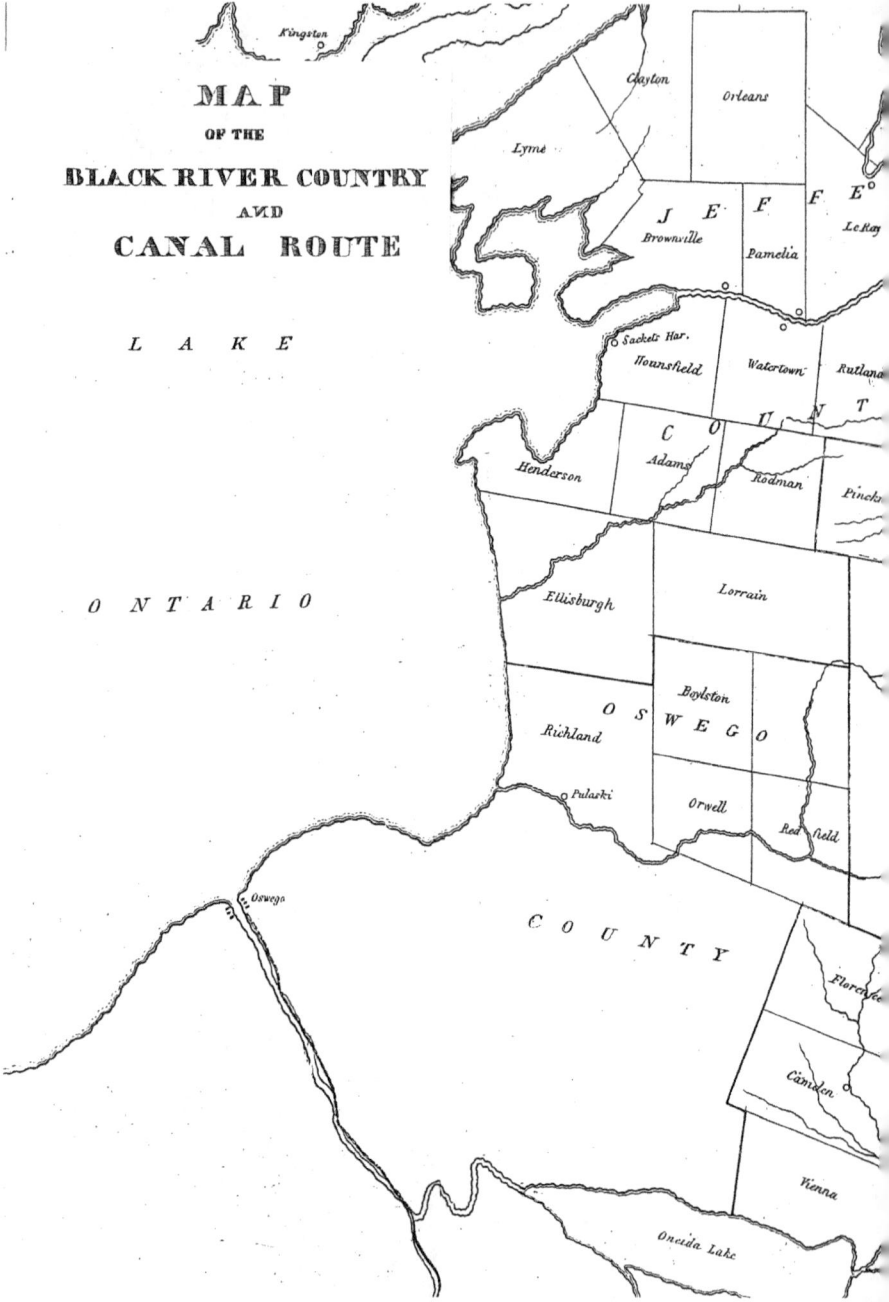

11. Map of the Black River region and proposed canal, showing Brown's

Tract and its subdivisions, outlined in pen by John Brown Francis.

12. Miniature portrait of Charles Frederick Herreshoff by Edward Greene Malbone, ca. 1800-01. (Courtesy Rhode Island Historical Society.)

13. "Herreshoff Manor," the house built by Charles Herreshoff on Brown's Tract, near Thendara, N.Y. (Courtesy The Adirondack Museum.)

14. First Lake, near Old Forge, N.Y. An anvil and trip hammer from Charles Herreshoff's forge were excavated here in the 1950s.

15. Sketch of Constable Hall, Constableville, N.Y. (Courtesy Constable Hall Association.)

16. An advertisement for stagecoach service in the *Albany Gazette,* 1810. (Courtesy New-York Historical Society.)

STAGES.

WESTERN LINE DAILY
FROM ALBANY TO UTICA.

17. Pomeroy's Tavern, Coventry, Conn. Now a private home.

18. Schenectady, N.Y., in the mid-1800s. Givens Hotel is at center left. (Courtesy Schenectady County Historical Society.)

19. Bennett's Light-house Tavern, Springfield, Mass.

20. Johnston Hall, Johnston, N.Y. (near Amsterdam). Built ca. 1749.

21. Water-driven tilt hammer, of the type used by Charles Herreshoff in manufacturing iron. From Overman's *The Manufacture of Iron*, 1850.

22. An early 20th-century postcard of the "Old Iron Mine at Fulton Chain. Opened by John Brown on John Brown's Tract. Here iron was mined that was forged at Old Forge."

HISTORY

OF THE

Rise, Progress, and existing Condition
OF THE
WESTERN CANALS
IN THE STATE OF NEW-YORK,

From September **1788**, to the completion of the
Middle Section of the

GRAND CANAL,

in 1819,

TOGETHER WITH THE
Rise, Progress, and existing State
OF
Modern Agricultural Societies,
On the Berkshire System,

From 1807, to the establishment of the Board of
Agriculture in the State of New-York,
January 10, 1820.

By *ELKANAH WATSON.*

Albany :
Published by D. Steele, No. 472 S. Market-street.
Packard & Van Benthuysen, Printers.

1820.

23. Elkanah Watson's *magnum opus.*

100 000
ACRES OF LAND,
For Sale.

THE subscriber, as the Agent of John B. Francis,

Esp. would wish to call the attention of the industrious farmer and mechanic to a tract of land, situated on the east side of Black River, in the counties of Lewis and Herkimer, about 12 miles from the flourishing villages of Lowville and Martinsburgh; and about 4 miles from Watson's settlement, where they have a grist and saw mill.

In giving a description of the land, the subscriber can say, that the growth of the timber on the arable land, is beech and maple—the face of the land level, or gently undulated : the soil a deep chocolate colored loam—remarkably well watered, having Beaver-river on the north, and Moose-river on the south part of the tract, with various tributary streams of pure excellent water.   Beaver-lake on the north part of the tract, is three miles long ; from one to two miles broad.   Lake Francis, 3 miles long, one mile broad, well stored with trout, salmon trout, and various other kinds of fish.   On the south part of the tract, are various other small pleasant lakes, well stored with fish.   The lakes and rivers have bold shores, and the whole tract very free from marshes or swamps.   The appearance of the soil is warm and friendly, and will be well adapted to all the staple articles of the state.   It has a less quantity of snow than is usual to this country, and it leaves it earlier in the spring.   A road is cut and worked from Lowville and Martinsburgh to the tract, passable for carriages, and various other roads are contracted to be made on, and through the tract this season.

The land will be sold to actual settlers, from one to two dollars per acre, on a liberal credit.— Those who pay 1-4 of the purchase money down, shall have six months without interest on the residue : Those who pay 1-2 down, one year's interest on the residue, and those who pay the whole down shall have one year's interest deducted from the purchase money.   The 30 first settlers on No. 2, and the 30 first settlers on No. 3, and the 30 first on any of the other towns, shall have their choice of the unsold lands on said towns, for one dollar per acre, and the other terms the same as above.   The subscriber will also take improved farms and stock.   To those who wish to purchase Townships, half or quarter towns, the prices will be reduced fifty per cent. with any credit wished for, if interest is paid annually, and promptly.

The owner's object in offering his lands for sale on such liberal terms, is to extend to settlers, a sufficient inducement for the purpose of effecting a permanent settlement of industrious and respectable men, however poor : but to the idle and dissipated he has no lands to sell.

A settlement has already commenced on the north, and one on the south parts of the tract.

Contracts will be given for deeds, and when the purchase money is paid, a clear and indisputable title, with warrantee, free from all incumbrance, will be given by the subscriber, at his office in the Village of Lowville.

ALSO, as the Agent of M. Le Ray de Chaumont, the subscriber offers for sale a Township of Land, a few miles from the village of Lowville, situated there on Chrystal Creek and Beaver River, for three dollars per acre, and seven years credit : the land is perhaps as good as any in the Black-river country, being a dark chocolate colored loam, well watered.   Roads will be cut through the Township this season.   The timber is beech, maple, elm, bass-wood, white ash, white oak, shag bark, walnut, butternut, &c. &c.

A number of improved farms for sale in the County of Lewis, on reasonable terms.

CHARLES DAYAN, *Agent.*

Lowville, Lewis Co. June 2d, 1821.

L. G. HOFFMAN, PRINTER—LOWVILLE.

24. An 1821 broadside attempting to attract settlers to Brown's Tract.

25. This 1833 portrait of Governor John Brown Francis by John N. Arnold hangs in the Rhode Island State House, Providence.

PART III - 1818

October 2, 1818
Left Providence on the 31st August 1818, taken with a fever on the 1st September confined to the bed 25 days.[1]

Left Brookfield on the 1st October 1818.

Lodged at Clapps in Belchertown—21 miles. Next day rode to Amherst to see a review, lodged at Northampton—15 miles from B[elchertown].

3rd
Rode in the afternoon to Worthington—20 miles, 1/2 way up hill. Pierce an excellent house.

4th
Lodged in Nassau state of NYK at Roots—36 miles up hill.

5th
In the morn'g rode to Albany—cold & uncomfortable weather.

6th
In the evn'g stopped at Givens in Schenectady[2]—cold.

---

1. As noted on page 79, Francis was cared for by "Doctor John Homans and Dr. Rice." Dr. Tilly Rice (1752-1824) of Brookfield served as captain of the 4th regiment of the Massachusetts militia during the Revolutionary War. He was admitted as a physician by Worcester County in 1806, and served as a justice of the peace in Brookfield for many years. Less is known about Dr. John Holman, except that he and his wife, Lucia Ruggles, and his brother-in-law served as medical missionaries in the Sandwich Islands (now Hawaii).

2. In 1817 Resolve Givens purchased the stagecoach tavern formerly known as the "old Beal." On his grand tour of the country in 1824, the Revolutionary War general Marquis de Lafayette was enthusiastically celebrated at the tavern, described as "accommodating 130 guests and furnished in a superior style, having a grand salon." It was destroyed by fire in 1843 and rebuilt as Givens Hotel.

7th

Over an infernal road to Midges—38 miles.

8th

Road better—dined at Morgans, Littlefalls³—supped at Baggs in Utica⁴—42 miles—horse not much wearied.

---

3. Morgan's Tavern was one of four taverns listed at the village of Little Falls, a busy stopover for the westward flow of settlers and commercial traffic on the Mohawk Turnpike and Inland Canal (later part of the Erie Canal). A traveler and author named John Melish was so impressed with the profusion of breakfast food and table accoutrements at Morgan's in 1811 that he itemized them all, with a little editorializing thrown in:

> The insertion of this will show that the people who live in the
> *back woods* are not quite so much in the savage state as some late
> tourists would have us to believe.

Table and table-cloth,	Sugar,
Tea-tray,	Cream,
Two metal tea-pots,	Bread,
One metal milk-pot,	Butter,
Sugar-bowl,	Toast and butter,
China cups,	Beef-steak,
Egg-cup,	Eggs,
Silver sugar-tongs,	Cheese,
Silver tea-spoons,	Crackers,
Silver castor, with 6 cut	Potatoes,
crystal glasses,	Beets,
Plates,	Salt,
Carving knife and fork,	Vinegar,
and common knife and fork,	Black pepper,
Tea,	Cayenne pepper

4. Bagg's Hotel, originally a log tavern built by Moses Bagg, was rebuilt as a hotel in 1813. The recollections of a visitor named Archibald Maxwell in 1840 show that the trappings of civilization didn't always correspond with genteel behavior:

> This house is magnificently fitted up, and admirably regulated,
> and leaves nothing to complain of but the abominable *fastness of
> their feasts*. Really, if I had not been initiated into the national habit,
> I should have imagined...that the parties pitted against each other
> had determined to settle the Presidential contest by eating instead

9th

In Utica Mr. B[rown] takes stage for Niagara—goes at 2 in the morn'g.

10th

Leave Utica alone & dine at Trenton—13 miles. Road very good—then to Boonville 18 miles. Eaton the Tavern keeper—a good house.

11th Octo Sunday

Dined & drank tea with [John L.] Post.
   [*Written in ink:*] Eliza's second Daughter born in September.

12th

Post leaves this [Boonville] with a drove of 112 cattle for Phila—a fine drove. Cattle as high here as in R.I.—price of driving 22/ a head.

13th

Col. Mappa arrived yesterday. I supped with him at Schuylers. A pleasant old gent. N[icholas] Vincent comes from the Tract with a horse for me to ride there. All well.

14th Wednesday

Rode to the tract—leave B[oonville] one quarter before 11 & reach Mr H[erreshoff] not before 6 or 7—road bad. Rain this day for the first time since I left Brookfield.

---

of voting.
   Both sides of an immensely long table were crowded with people, stuffing themselves as if for life or death. I never before beheld such a gormandizing struggle! I at length got a place, and sat down in the midst of them, to view their operations and eat my dinner; but, before I had finished my soup, the whole party, as if by magic, had vanished, and, alas! the viands with them!

15th

N[icholas] Brown Jun'r5 surprised us by his presence this Even'g. He had no conception of the distance or state of the road or not a bribe would have got him here.

16th

Fine weather yet Mr. H remarks that he has always seen snow before this—sometimes it has cover'd the ground for whole days nay once for a week in Octo. This season is as mild as any one could desire. With Mr. H. & N[icholas] B[rown] go to the mills. I on horse-back in consideration of bad health.

Mr. H. invention for cleaning ore a very ingenious one— a cylinder the size of a beer barrel is coated with a thousand magnets.[6]

It is put in motion (a very slow one) by a water power—as it turns, the ore is attracted by the magnet & then drops off.

The ore falls on the cylinder thro' a hopper.

This operation must be repeated twice as some of the ore is not separated the first time.

The cylinder is free from the ore by a brush.

Mr. H. thinks with six cylinders one revolving under the other he could clean two thousand pounds a day.

---

5. Nicholas Brown (1792-1859) was the eldest son of Nicholas Brown Jr. and first cousin of John Brown Francis, who cordially despised him as spoiled and pompous. He graduated from Brown University (named for his father) in 1811, served as President Polk's Consul to Rome in 1846-48, and was elected Lieutenant Governor of Rhode Island in 1856, under Governor Elisha Dyer.

6. Richard Sanders Allen of Albany, a historian of the early iron industry in New England and New York, wrote in a 1988 letter to Henry A.L. Brown, "The primary separation of iron from raw ore was a problem which the early bloomery forge operators of northern New York tackled in several ways and with varying degrees of success. Iron lumps and grains, being heavier, would gravitate to the bottom of the first crude crushers. Sometimes they were laboriously shaken down and hand-picked by workmen.

It has been found to make iron (high) being passed thro' the hopper twice—but if by six operations, which by the size, requires no more labor if you have that number of cylinders than one in the present machine, he can produce <u>pure ore</u>.

This is great in theory at any rate—

Dine on venison, take tea with Mr. Brown—pies such as would do credit to R.I.

17th

Mr. Brown goes out with a party of Welchmen. An unusually blustering day. Mr. H's sheep reduced to a flock of less than 100.7

18th Sunday—Octo 1818

A delightful day—men return from Alder Creek without fish—

"Eventually a series of tumbling barrels was evolved and the ore was washed. The proprietors of ironworks in upstate New York had a singular advantage: their ore was of the magnetic variety and men were quick to see the possibilities of using magnetic force in the separation of the iron from the crushed raw ore.

"At Franconia in the White Mountains of New Hampshire, an isolated iron works had been established in 1811, using magnetic ores from a mine in nearby Lisbon. Connected with this enterprise was Samuel Browning, who, on October 13, 1812, patented the first 'magnetic cylinder' [on] the principle of separating iron from crushed ore by the use of magnetized steel....Two years later he was granted another patent...for an improved model.

"Except for the original New Hampshire application, the 'cleaning barrel' set up by Charles Frederick Herreshoff on Moose River in Brown's Tract is the first and earliest mention of a magnetic iron ore separator put to use (at least in the Northeast). Whether Herreshoff knew of Browning's patent, adapted and used it, or whether he devised [it] entirely on his own cannot now be ascertained."

In 1836, Governor John Brown Francis received a letter from James H. Rogers and Joseph Goulding seeking information on Herreshoff's device for use in a patent dispute in a U.S. court. They were attempting to prove that the Herreshoff iron ore separator had predated one for which a patent was claimed—which suggests that the device was, if not the first of its kind, one of the earliest used in that region.

7. See n. 4, Part II.

water too low.

A cloudless night.

19th

Ice a quarter of an inch thick this morn'g—clear & pleasant.

The Bloomers employed in getting ore from the quarry.[8]

Mr. H. tried an experiment yesterday to clean the ore by throwing it in the flume at the mill. The current floated the light stone & earth some distance whilst the heavy ore sunk directly.

This appears a very simple manner of separating these materials.

The ore in Salisbury Con't costs $5 a ton and 5 tons make only one ton of iron—iron sells for $120.

$$
\begin{array}{lll}
\text{ore at} & 25 \text{ Dr} & \\
\text{coal "} & 27 \text{ "} & 600 \text{ bushels for a ton} \\
& & \text{cost } 4\text{-}1/2 \text{ for } 100 \\
\text{labor—} & \underline{25} & \\
& \$64 &
\end{array}
$$

Mr. H. says that his iron will cost him no more than this the ton & that he can sell it at the forge for 140 Dr. This leaves the enormous profit of 82 Drs & 2 tons may be made with two fires every week!!

164 Dr a week!!

---

8. Richard Sanders Allen (see n. 6 above) writes in the same letter, "The bloomery forges of the Adirondacks were, in general, blessed with exceedingly rich magnetic ores, varying from 30% to 60% pure iron. As it came from the ground, the ore was first crushed and separated to remove as much sand, rock and other material as possible from the grains of iron. Then it was heated in small charcoal furnaces (or 'forges'), stirred into a pasty mass called a 'loupe' and beaten with water-powered triphammers to remove impurities. The battered loupe was then re-heated and re-beaten as many times as necessary and finally forged into a 'bloom,' or billet. The end result was surprisingly pure wrought iron of much usefulness. It could be cut into bars and then again re-heated, beaten and forged to make hundreds of iron products."

There can be no fluctuation in the demands for iron. It must be eternally an article of the first necessity—hence the saying that ironmongers never become bankrupt. Their goods never go out of fashion.

<u>If the ore is found in plenty</u> & of the same quality that has received such universal praise, nothing can prevent Mr. H's success & he richly deserves it.

Octo 20th

The ore has been burnt today. Tomorrow it is to be pounded & washed in the flume & on thursday they expect to make a Loup.

Read Judge Reeves9 title of Mortgages.

My anxiety to see iron made here is the cause of my detention. Heaven knows how anxious I am to see home.

Octo 21st

Rains violently but clears off by 2 o'clk. Walk to the mills. The longest walk I have attempted since my sickness.

The young woman at Thomas's10 fell thro' the floor whilst I was there into the family apartment! She was not a little abashed but not otherwise incommoded.

---

9. Tapping Reeves (b. 17?) was born on Long Island, graduated with honors from Princeton College in 1763, and married Sally Burr, granddaughter of Rev. Jonathan Edwards, the famous Puritan minister, and sister of Aaron Burr. Reeves studied law under Judge Jesse Root, and was admitted to the bar of Litchfield County, Connecticut, in 1772. His law office in Litchfield eventually formed the nucleus of a law school in 1774, and Reeves erected a separate building near his house where classes were held. Graduates included Moses Brown Ives (1812), John Brown Francis (1813) and John C. Calhoun, later Vice President and Secretary of State. Reeves retired in 1820 and his partner James Gould in 1833, after which the law school closed down.

10. Silas Thomas, a settler on the Tract, became agent for Brown's Tract after Charles Herreshoff's suicide in 1819. Like the other agents since John Brown's time, Thomas apparently had little success attracting settlers to the area.

Lothrop an old man, occupies [Major] Joy's house. His son-in-law James Deth bo't the lot for 500 Dr.—now absent.

Schneider a German, writes from Long Island that he is coming here—wants the Clark farm.

Told Mr. H. that he might offer the wild land at 2 Drs [an acre] & the cleared at any price fixed on by competent & impartial judges. This doesn't include the Leach clearing.

22 Octo

Awakened often unseasonable hour by the pelting of hail & snow ag'st the glass. It became cold after the rain yesterday & this morn'g the earth is cover'd with snow.

The storm abated before meridian but flakes of snow fell thro' the day.

Keep the house, the walking being intolerably bad & the air too chilly for comfort.

Morgan the hunter, comes in—the weather was "too eternal" for thin breeches.

The poor devil must have passed a miserable night. The life of a hunter has no attractions for me save what it partakes of independ'cy.

These two fellows, Morgan & White, are said to have taken skins each to the value of 250 Dr. Beaver & Muskrats Martins Minks & Otters the last used for caps.

23rd

Cold & wintry—snow on the ground all day—go to the forge & witness for the first time the manufacture of iron. Passed a very tedious day burning on one side & freezing on the other—but a loup—the technical name for the iron that may be made (a corruption as I suppose of lump) was taken out just before night & put under the trip hammer. The iron of the same quality with all that has been made—its weight about 84 [lbs.].

Mr. H. says 3 hours is long enough for a blast & that 3 loups may be formed in a day—but double that time was consumed in the formation of this.

24th
Cold but pleasant. Appearances favorable at the mine so says Mr. H. Snow still on the earth.

25th Sunday—October 1818
Weather so warm as to be more pleasant in the shade than the sun. Walk to the mill to see the iron which they yesterday stomped into bars. It has the same appearance of the sample I have seen before. Swedes iron is probably inferior. This is saying enough in its praises. The bloomers made another loup yesterday. "They never saw ore work more kindly"—4 cwt can be obtained from one piece in a day—but this is a large calculation. 3 Loups is a days work & 1 cwt heavy enough for a Loup.

Mr. H. is more confident than ever today that the ore such as he is in search of (so pure as not to need washing) is within a weeks drilling which may God in his mercy grant. Supposed 2 stout horses may carry 10 cwt thro' the woods on a sled—

doubted—

Fuller says 500 bushels of coal is as much as [he] wants for a ton of iron.

Thomas is now burning 20,000 of coal at 4-1/2 Dr—They will make 40 tons of iron which Mr. H. hopes to see before he sees Rhode Island.

The forge is a substantial building. fact by & is pronounced by judges to be remarkably well contrived.

I regret [the] vicinity of my mill on acc't of fire. There is said to be water for eight forges—or in fact double that number.

The privilege combines all requisites.

No person ever saw one better & perhaps in all respects so good.

[*Written in pencil:*] bloomer one fifth the value of the iron.

Monday 26 October 1818

With G. Vincent & Roda—G on foot depart for Boonville.

G paces all the bad places between the old clearing & Moose river makes 50 rods of logways necessary.

G found it difficult to keep our company—he ran several miles.

27

Smoky weather an indication of the Indian Summer.

Wrote an agreement for Wheeler to make 50 rods of cross ways which I left with the Capt for W's signature.

Offered 9/ a rod but W & Brum refused it.

28

Get into the chaise at 10 o'clk—destination Stephen Smith's.

Road abominably bad, the greater part of the way—Reach Smith's not before dark. Dined at Hughes in Remsen—a Welchman. He made a prayer in that lingo at the table of nearly 15 minutes in length. 300 Welch are said to have settled in this vicinity this season all from Wales.

Crops abundant thro' the country—S[mith] raised the Indian Corn for the first time these three years. 180 bushels from 4 acres of land—new land.

Weather cold enough for Jan'y—a few flakes of snow.

Russia October 29th 1818

Leave the house of Smith where I have been hospitably entertained.

12 [noon]

This day for my **native land** & with a very light heart. The thought of seeing <u>the world</u> there inspires me in a manner, not the most agreeable to my nag. Over a bad road a part of the way at least I rode 28 miles to Palantine. W. Lapell the Taverner, orig. from Prov. & a clever fellow—post master etc. etc. gave me money to pay old Dods[11] for barberries.

The Country hilly, free from stones & fertile. This most delightful one to visit at some distant day. The land now cleared with scarcely any interruption on each side of the road & the stumps are disappearing.

Passed a number of emigrants on their way to LeRoy[12] & then St. Lawrence.

30th Octo

12 miles to Johnstown—road very rough—land timber'd with pine.

Again pass the seat Sir William[13]—one mile west of the town.

The fields in this part of the world peculiarly smooth, entirely free of hillocks as well as stones. The rise seldom abrupt. I have seen no level land nor any waste—fruit trees vigorous—apples in any quantity.

6 miles from J. to Tribes hill where you intersect the Mohawk

---

11. "Old Dods" was the cooper employed by Francis's aunt, Sarah Brown Herreshoff, at the Point Pleasant estate in Bristol, Rhode Island.

12. The LeRays were wealthy French slave traders who owned vast acreage in both New York and Pennsylvania. Jacques LeRay and his brother-in-law Paul Chassanis (see n. 34, part I) originally purchased the New York lands from William Constable. Jacques' son, James LeRay de Chaumont, had an opulent stone chateau built near Watertown, which is now the residence of the commanding general of the Camp Drum military reservation.

13. William Johnston (1715-1774), born in Ireland, came to America around 1738 to oversee property inherited from his uncle. He married a Native American woman named Mary, sister of Joseph Brant, chief of the Mohawks' Thayendanegea tribe. Johnston was awarded a 100,000-acre tract of land by King George II and named "sole superintendent of the Six [Indian] Nations" for forming an alliance with the Indian tribes in an expedition against the French at Lake George in 1755. He was knighted by the King, served as colonial agent for the Crown, and made a sachem of the Mohawk tribe. Before Sir William died in 1774, his son succeeded him as Indian agent. When he and his Indian allied forces were defeated fighting for the Crown during the Revolutionary War, the family's baronial estate in Johnston, New York, was forfeited to the State of New York.

road—a chaise is not the vehicle for the Black river route—in wet weather it would be impracticable to go with one—now the holes of some of the ruts may be shunned.

A logway is a severe trial for the rider too as well as the chaise. Dine in Amsterdam & lodge at Schenectady. 30 or 40 miles.

The first 12 miles intolerably hilly & rough & the last 18 sandy & stony.

Every third house as a moderate calculation on my route so far has offer'd entertainment "for man & horse."

31 Octo
Over an execerable road 15 miles to Albany—stop at Bairds. Went directly to the Post Office rec'd 3 letters from my mother— one from aunt F[isher] one from Mr. Harrison & one from Capt. Schuyler.

The atmosphere has been smokey for the last 4 or 5 days—it's been attributed to fires in the Catskill range. Saw at the museum a bottle s'd to be taken from the ship sunk in the sound in the rev. war. It was covr'd with oyster shells of a larger size & contained wine—many bottles are said to have retained all the wine & in perfection but this was not a third full & the wine has lost its virtue.

Albany Sunday Nov 1 1818
Employed in making off the acc't to the Comptroller. Wrote Aunt Fisher & M[oses] B[rown] I[ves].

Nov 2
Somewhat derangé ce matine—Comptroller puts me off to two o'clk & had then only time to listen to a few explanations. Thinks that the acc't may be settled & promises to send it to Prov as soon as it has been examined.

Bal: due the com[ptroller] about 95 Drs.

Drew on order for one hundred for which was p'd me by Cox the Treasurer.

Saw E[lkanah] Watson—he talks of nothing but cattle shows & canals & seems really beside himself.[14]

Conversed with a Mr. Briggs a Quaker from Penn probably one of the officers employed by the state the chief surveyor I suspect.

He says if the state will grant the sum which it contemplates granting in the space of ten years in five years that the whole canal may be completed.[15]

The middle section from Utica to Seneca River a distance of 93 miles will be in readiness for boats next season.

The boats to carry from 30 to 35 tons—but the locks to be broad enough to admit of one hundred tons. There is this section a distance of 50 miles on the same level. The northern Canal will not be completed next season—but they are at work on it.

Albany is a place of perpetual bustle—the main street has all the air of a city—shops without number & supplied on an extensive scale.

But the spirit of the inhabitants now depressed. Prospects are s'd to be not the most flattering. This Canal which is to enrich so many may they apprehend impoverish them. The western country & NYK city will enjoy the highest benefits.

---

14. See n. 13, part I.

15. The Erie Canal had its beginnings in 1791, when the New York legislature appointed Gen. Philip Schuyler, who had just completed a term in the U.S. Senate, Elkanah Watson, and Goldsbrow Banyar to survey a route for an inland waterway from the Hudson River to the Great Lakes. All three men were avid promoters of internal improvements; Watson had already traversed the Mohawk route as a possible canal route in 1788. They submitted a survey report in 1792 outlining a route from Albany to Buffalo. Work began immediately at both ends of the canal, known simply as the Grand Canal. At Little Falls, a bypass around the rapids was completed in 1795, and the canal at Rome, connecting the Mohawk River and Lake Ontario, was completed in 1797. The first canal boat was "drag'd" by a single horse from Rome to Utica on October 22, 1819. After DeWitt Clinton, a canal enthusiast, became Governor of New York in 1817, the legislature voted enough money to allow the Erie Canal (as it was renamed) to be completed by 1825.

Left A this eve'g at sunset in order to get a fair start in the morn'g.

Nov. 3

Rode to Stockbridge—first part of the way hilly—34 [miles] from Albany. Latter part smooth as a bowling green—it is impossible to conceive of a smoother road. A good house at S[tockbridge]. My horse fell an broke one of the thills. Saw one of the candidates for Congress, Col Dwight a fine figure of a man. It is tho't there is no election. This in Berkshire Mass.

13 miles to the top of the mountains—lodge at an ordinary looking house kept by Heeter. No bad hills have I seen & yet I am at the summit & have no more mountains to rise this trip—laud deo.

In this respect the route has a preference over the Northampton—

Tavern Keeper at S[tockbridge] remarkably civil & the very best ostler I have seen.

A miserable country the last 13 miles. Swamps & rocky hills covered with green timber. Near Otis few or no inhabitants.

I have noticed some sheep today, large enough for the Bakewell breed.

This a noted sheep country—they can be maintained as cheap as anywhere in this latitude.

The President of the agricultural society—Merrill has invented several implements of husbandry. E. Watson told me that among them he saw a harrow of a construction entirely new.

Berket & Otis grazing Towns. When I asked the Landlord if they raised corn this year his reply was that it was "easier to get a living out of a cows teats". He formerly made 90 barrels of cider & now only 3!!! Orchards have depreciated in the same propo: elsewhere on the mountains attributed to the coldness of the earth. On new land trees might grow but on old they perish with the cold. This landlord's theory.

4th Nov 1818

25 miles principally along the foot of mountains & descending them.

The course by the side of the river, highly romantic. The farmers get their wood simply by cutting, it tumbles into the water without further assistance.

The village of Chester pleasantly situated & Westfield more so, lodged at Bennetts[16] in Springfield.

The ride delightful this side of Chester. At that place you may retrace y'r route over the mountain. There are three & I have travelled them all. The last perhaps the nearest & for aught I know the least mountainous.

200 men at work in S[pringfield] fabricating arms for the U.S.[17] The space the U.S. occupy ceded by the State. None of the artisans allowed to intermeddle in State affairs. The votes of S. once thrown out because this rule was violated.

An appearance of wealth in this place. Houses superb or intending to be so at least.

5th Nov.

I imprudently left off my coat yesterday & took cold & a more wreached night scarcely ever passed. My kidnies were effected. I attribute this to my posture in the chaise & to a see saw motion.

10 miles over a plain cover'd with scrub pine or fields of rye—no fencing. Leave the Boston road 14 miles from S. in Pelham for Brim-

---

16. John Bennett's tavern on Court Square, "18 feet north of the great elm," was visited by George Washington in 1783.

17. The Springfield Armory was first authorized by the Continental Congress in 1778 on a site chosen by George Washington. The U.S. Congress officially established the armory in 1794. At the time Francis visited in 1818, it was producing 12,000 muskets a year, along with an assortment of rifles, pistols, carbines, musketoons, and other weaponry.

field. Smooth & rough alternately. This is the seat of Shays insurrection.[18] Now a florishing country. Many of the houses are old & in a state of delapitation, however some attention is occassionally bestowed on agricultural improvements but the general system of cropping dreadfully destructive.

Leave the county Hampden in Brimfield, pass into Sturbridge & lodge in Southfield, 11 miles & 36 from S. There is a rage throughout the Country for new meeting houses & for building costly dwelling houses. The mania of N. England—The manners of the people & the appearances of all the villages indicate cultivation & wealth.

The yeomanry are far beyond ours in R.I. in cultivation & they are without narrow prejudices & superstition of their Con[necticut] brethren. The State in larger matters are conducted on a more liberal scale & the country leading receive a polish & more enlarged views in their connection with the great men at the capital. They associate there with the most enlightened men of the day. In Connecticut there is a greater equality & thru' straightforward path for everyone to move in.

The poor know just enough to be pedantic & to harangue about State affairs in the most consequential & impertinant manner & Clergy with many pretensions indeed to knowledge are generally conceited, extremely outre in their manner & bigot to Connecticut [?] habit as they are called.

6th November in Prov. 1818

∽∽∽

---

18. Shays's Rebellion was a short-lived tax revolt in 1786-87, named for Daniel Shays, a former captain in the Continental Army who led an army of thousands of disaffected farmers to protest Massachusetts' high property taxes in the postwar depression. The protest turned violent, and Shays's army captured Worcester and Springfield before being routed by the state militia.

Notes in flyleaf of diary, Part III:

Brookfield
Worcester Co.
Massachusetts

Doctor John Homans & Dr. Rice Physicians

Palatine   Octo 30, 1818—Received of U. Lapell, Innkeeper at Lapell
three dollars for old Mr. Dods the cooper.

Silas Thomas	10.88
Southwell	3.64
Grant	38.16
Herreshoff	79.
Slocum	14.87
Thrasher	22.50
Sparcy	7
Bronson	9
Rowlin	24.50
Joy	410.
Smith	127.50
"	107.50
	$854.55
[?]	42.00
	$931.55
Brum	15.00
D.& I.	20.00
	$966.55
Joy	460.
Smith	235.
Slocum	14.87
Thomas	10.88

Thrasher	22.50
Sperry	7
Bronson	9
Southwell	3.64
Rowlin & Ives	24.50
Dibble	20.
Grant	_35._
	$842.39
	_79._
	$921.39

Debt of Mr. N[icholas] B[rown] Junr. somewhere about 180 or 200 Dr.

9th Octo
1818

At Bairds	$7.62
Horse	
Servants etc.	2.12
Toll	.20
7th at Givens	2.66
	.18
[?] & toll	.50
	.37
Midges	2.50
Tolls & others	.30
	1.36
	.36
	.25
	_.12_
	$18.73

Appendix A: John Brown Francis Genealogy

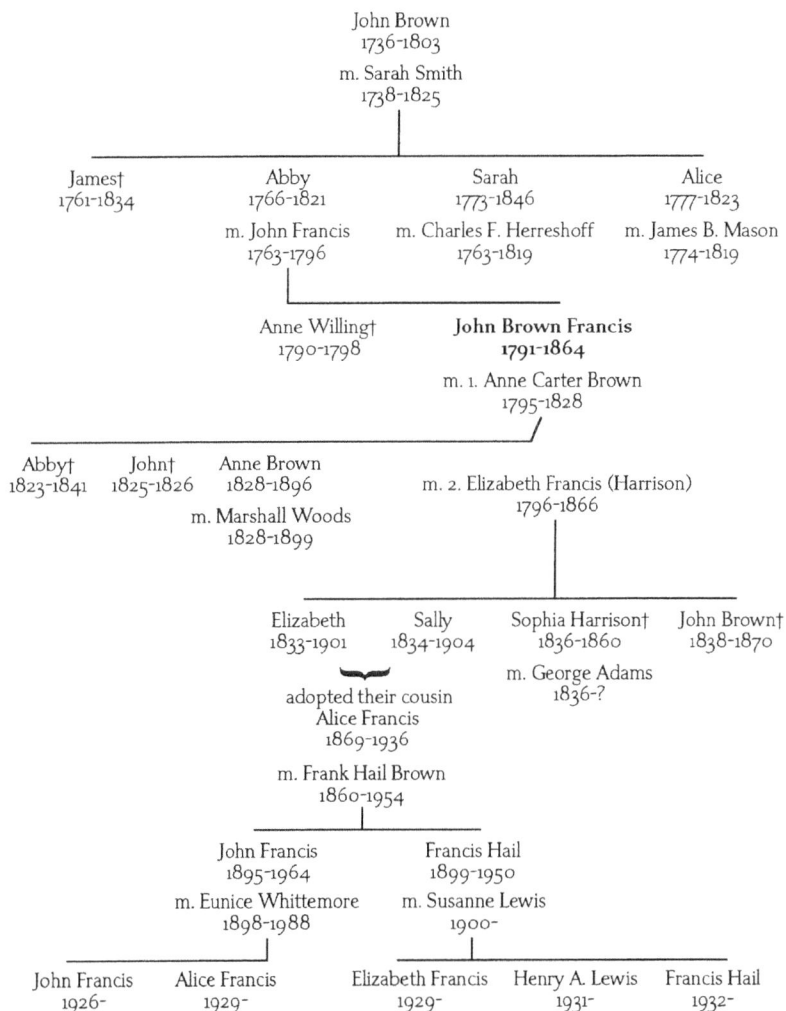

John Brown
1736-1803
m. Sarah Smith
1738-1825

James†	Abby	Sarah	Alice
1761-1834	1766-1821	1773-1846	1777-1823
	m. John Francis	m. Charles F. Herreshoff	m. James B. Mason
	1763-1796	1763-1819	1774-1819

Anne Willing†
1790-1798

John Brown Francis
1791-1864
m. 1. Anne Carter Brown
1795-1828

Abby†	John†	Anne Brown	
1823-1841	1825-1826	1828-1896	m. 2. Elizabeth Francis (Harrison)
		m. Marshall Woods	1796-1866
		1828-1899	

Elizabeth	Sally	Sophia Harrison†	John Brown†
1833-1901	1834-1904	1836-1860	1838-1870
		m. George Adams	
		1836-?	

adopted their cousin
Alice Francis
1869-1936
m. Frank Hail Brown
1860-1954

John Francis	Francis Hail
1895-1964	1899-1950
m. Eunice Whittemore	m. Susanne Lewis
1898-1988	1900-

John Francis	Alice Francis	Elizabeth Francis	Henry A. Lewis	Francis Hail
1926-	1929-	1929-	1931-	1932-

† Died without issue.

Appendix B: J.B. Francis's Travel Routes

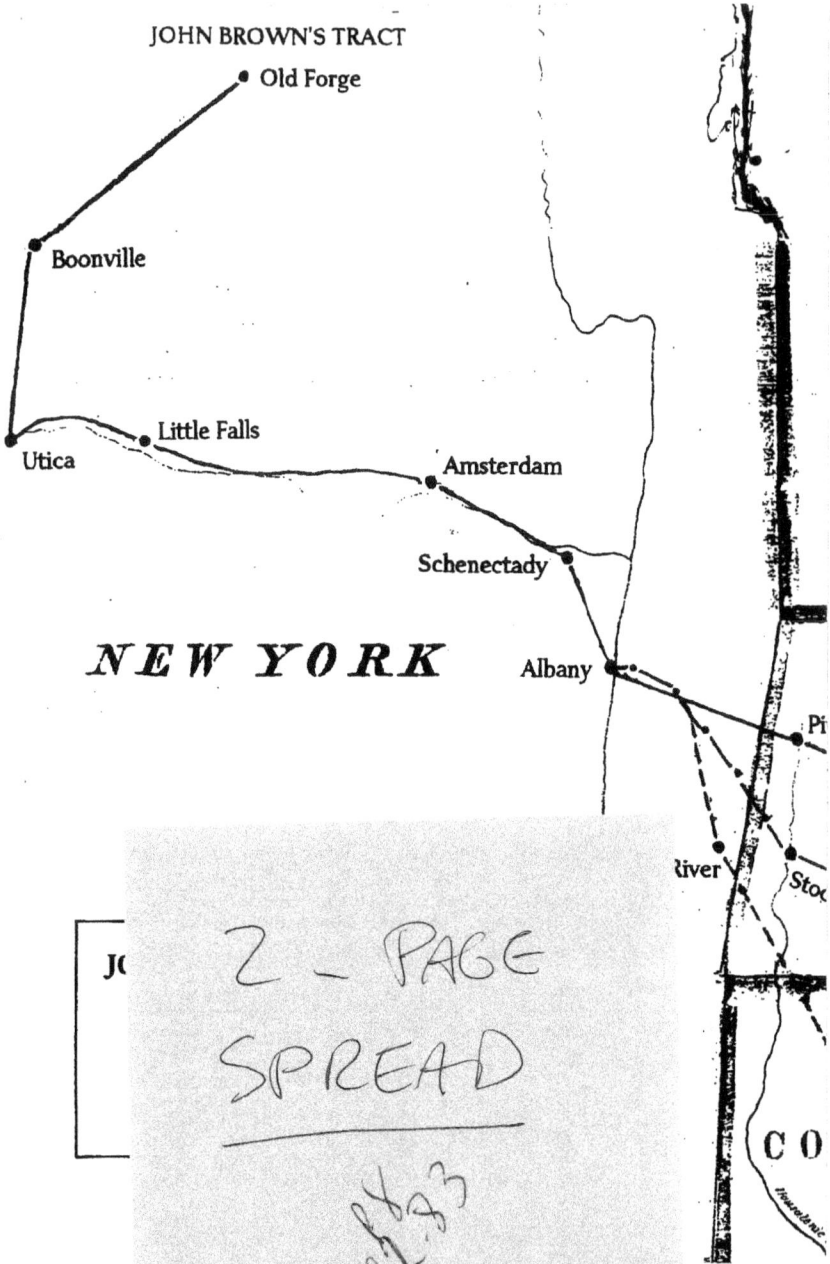

JOHN BROWN'S TRACT

Old Forge

Boonville

Little Falls

Utica

Amsterdam

Schenectady

NEW YORK

Albany

River

Sto

C O

2 – PAGE SPREAD

NDIXES

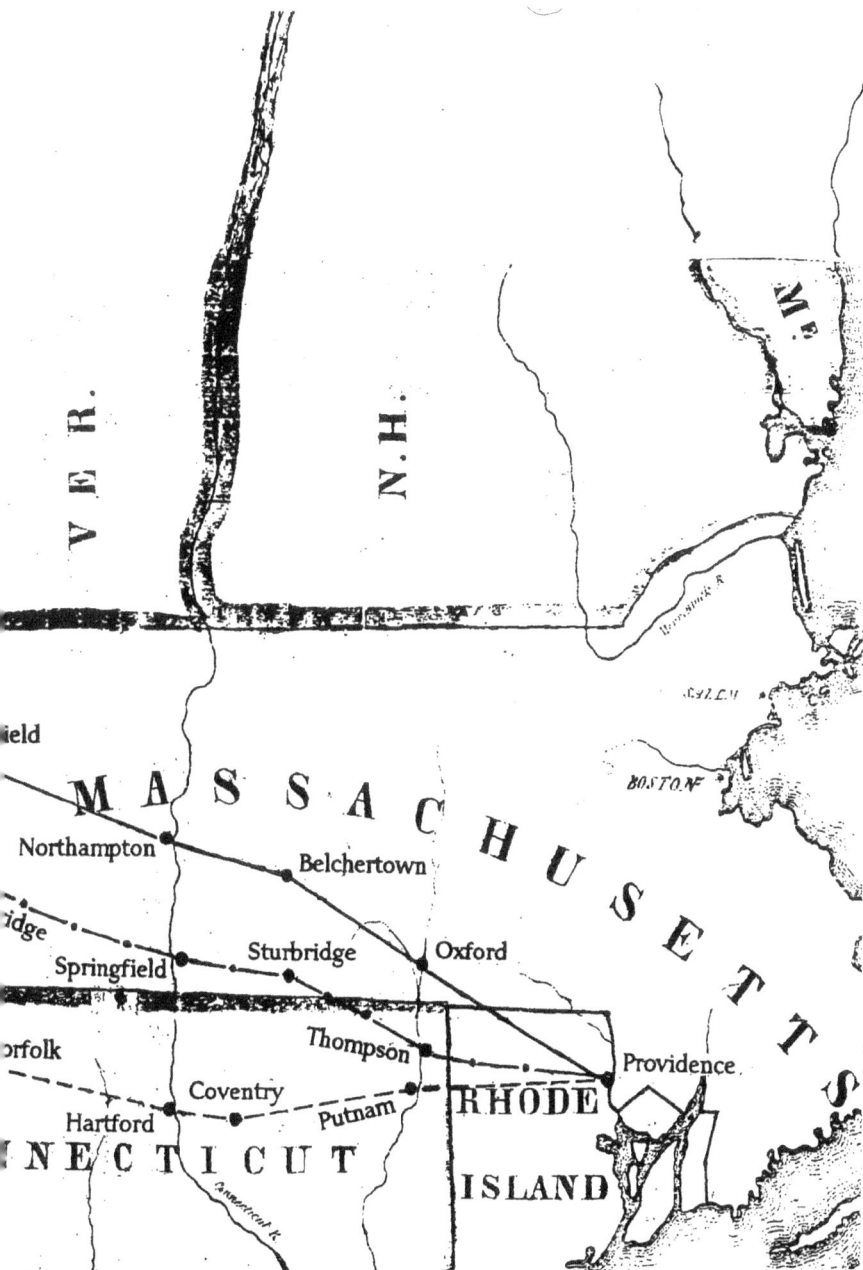

VER.

N.H.

ME.

MASS.

BOSTON

ield

MASSACHUSETTS

Northampton

Belchertown

idge

Springfield

Sturbridge

Oxford

orfolk

Thompson

Providence

Coventry

Putnam

RHODE

Hartford

NECTICUT

ISLAND

BIBLIOGRAPHY

Albany Directory, 1817. Albany, N.Y.: Pachard & van Pently, 1817.

Allen, Richard Sanders. Letter to Henry A.L. Brown. 21 September 1988.

Angell, Avery F. *Genealogy of the Descendants of Thomas Angell who settled in Providence, 1636.* Providence: A.C. Greene, 1872.

Angell, James K. Letters to John Brown Francis. 9 July 1820 and 25 August 1821.

Bagg, M.M. *Memorial History of Utica, N.Y.* Syracuse, N.Y.: D. Mason & Co., 1892.

Baldwin, Charles. *Universal Biographical Dictionary.* New York, 1825.

Baum, Gerald R. "Tavern Life In Upstate New York." Unpublished thesis. Cooperstown (N.Y.) Graduate Programs, 1976.

Blake, Charles. *An Historical Account of the Providence Stage.* Providence: George Whitney, 1868.

Blake, J.L. *Blake's Biographical Dictionary.* Boston, 1854.

Bresnahan, Shaw. *Vision of a Time Past: Belchertown 1790-1840.* Southbridge, Mass.: Paquette Stationery Co., 1983.

Brookfield Town Records of Deaths and Marriages. Brookfield, Mass. *Brookfield Historical Commission Survey Report.* Brookfield, Mass., 1988.

Brown, Henry A.L. and Walton, Richard J. *John Brown's Tract: Lost Adirondack Empire.* Providence: Rhode Island Historical Society, 1988.

Bulkey, Isabel Brown. *The Chad Browne Memorial. Brooklyn Daily Eagle,* 1888.

Carpenter, Frank. "Paradise Held: William Ellery Channing and the Legacy of Oakland." *Newport History,* vol. 65, part 3, no. 224, 1994.

Chambers' Encyclopaedia, A Dictionary of Universal Knowledge For the People. London: Ward K. Chambers, 1876.

Child, Hamilton. *Gazetteer of Berkshire County.* Syracuse, N.Y.: Journal Office, 1885.

-- *Gazetteer and Business Directory of Columbia County, New York.* Syracuse: Journal Office, 1871.

-- *Gazetteer and Business Directory of Lewis County, New York.* Syracuse: Journal Office, 1873.

Clapp Memorial. Belchertown, N.Y., 1876.

Collins, Clarkson A. 3rd. "The Patrol of Narragansett Bay, 1774-76."
  Rhode Island History, vol. 7, no. 1, Jan. 1948; vol. 7, no. 3, July 1948;
  vol. 8, no. 2, Apr. 1949; vol. 8, no. 3, July 1949; vol. 9, no. 1, Jan. 1950;
  vol. 9, no. 2, Apr. 1950.
Cooney, Edward J. *Little Falls Diamond Jubilee*. Little Falls, N.Y., 1970.
Daniels, George F. *History of Oxford Massachusetts*. Oxford, 1892.
Dennis, Frederic S. *The Village Green*. Norfolk, Conn., 1917.
Dickinson, Doris. "Belchertown" in *The Hampshire History*.
  Northampton, Mass., 1964.
Dictionary of National Biography. London and New York:Oxford
  University Press, 1975.
Donaldson, Alfred L. *History of the Adirondacks*. New York: Century, 1921.
Earle, Alice M. *Stage Coach and Tavern Days*. New York: Macmillan, 1900.
Ellis, David M. "Rise of the Empire State, 1790-1820." *New York History*,
  vol. 56, no. 1, January 1975.
Federal Writers' Project of the W.P.A. for the State of Connecticut.
  Cambridge: Riverside Press, 1938.
Federal Writers' Project of the W.P.A. for the State of Rhode Island.
  Cambridge: Riverside Press, 1937.
Field, Edward. *State of Rhode Island and Providence Plantations at
  the End of the Century: A History*. Boston: Mason Publishing, 1902.
Fisher, Maj. Gen. Carlton E. and Fisher, Sue Gray. *Soldiers and
  Patriots of the Revolutionary War, Vermont*. Camden, Me.: Picton
  Press, 1992.
Fry, J. *Annual Register and Albany Register*. Albany, 1815.
Hedges, James B. *The Browns of Providence Plantations*. Providence:
  Brown University Press, 1952.
Hislop, Codman. *Eliphalet Nott*. Middletown, Conn.: Wesleyan
  University Press, 1971.
Hough, Franklin B. *History of Lewis County*. Albany: Munsell &
  Rowland, 1860.
Howison, John. *Sketches of Upper Canada, Domestic, Local, and
  Characteristic: To which are Added, Practical Details for the
  Information of Emigrants of every class: and some Recollections of
  the United States of America*. Reprint of 1821 ed. New York: Johnson
  Reprint Corporation, 1965.
Jerome, Christine. *An Adirondack Passage: The Cruise of the Canoe*

Sairy Gamp. New York: Harper Collins, 1994.

Keith, Charles P. *Provincial Councillors of Pennsylvania*. Trenton, N.J.:
W.S. Sharp Printing, 1883.

Kennedy, Roger G. *Orders From France*. New York: Alfred A. Knopf, 1989.

King, Moses. *Springfield, Massachusetts*. Springfield: James D. Gill, 1884.

Lathrop, Elsie. *Early American Inns and Taverns*. New York: Robert
McBrice & Co., 1926.

Levaillant, Maurice. "Napoleon and the Femmes Fatales." *Horizons*,
vol. 1, no. 2, Nov. 1958.

Linchlaen, John. *Travels in the years 1791 and 1792 in Pennsylvania,
New York and Vermont*. New York and London: G. P. Putnam's
Sons, 1897.

Lippincott, J.B. *Geographical Dictionary of the World*. Philadelphia: J.B.
Lippincott & Co., 1883.

Lossing, Benson J. *Harper's Popular Cyclopaedia of United States
History*. New York: Harper & Brothers, 1893.

Massachusetts Soldiers of the Revolutionary War. Boston: Wright
& Potter Printing Co., 1905.

Malone, D., ed. *Dictionary of American Biography*. New York: Charles
Scribner & Sons, 1934.

McKenna, Marian C.. *Tapping Reeves and the Litchfield Law
School*. New York, London, Rome: Oceana Publications, 1986.

New England Genealogical Registry. Boston, 1907.

O'Callaghan, E.B. *Documentary History of the State of New York*.
Albany: Weed, Parsons & Co., 1849.

*The Official Reports of the Canal Commissioners of the State of New
York, and the Navigable Communications between the Great Western
and Northern Lakes and the Atlantic Ocean; with perspicuous Maps
and Profiles*. Newburgh (N.Y.): B.F. Lewis & Shelton & Kenesett
(Ward M. Gazlay, Printer), August 1817.

Overman, Frederick. *The Manufacture of Iron*. Philadelphia: Henry
C. Baird, 1850.

Pierce, Clarence E. *Thurber Family Records*. East Providence, R.I., 1930.

Pilcher, Edith. *Castorland*. Harrison, N.Y.: Harbor Hill Books, 1985.

Reid, Max W.. *The Mohawk Valley*. New York: G.P. Putnam's Sons, 1901.

Report of Patents for the Year 1849. U.S. Senate document no. 15.
Washington, D.C.: Office of Printers to the Senate, 1850.

Rice, Franklin P. *Vital Records of Brookfield, Mass.* Boston: Stanhope Press, 1909.

Rogers, L.E. *Biographical Cyclopaedia of Representative Men of Rhode Island.* Providence: National Biographical PublishingCo., 1881.

Shepard, Henry L. *Litchfield.* Litchfield, Conn.: G. Wilson, 1969.

Simister, Florence Parker. "Rhode Island Exodus: IV New York State, 1797: John Brown's Tract." *Rhode Island Yearbook 1971,* pp. 12-16. Providence: R.I. Yearbook Foundation, 1970.

Smith, A.E. *History of Pittsfield, 1800-1876.* Springfield, Mass.: C.W. Bryan & Co., 1876.

Snyder, Charles B. "John Brown's tract." An address to the Herkimer County (N.Y.) Historical Society, December 8, 1896.

Spafford, Horatio Gates. *A Pocket Guide for the Tourist and Traveller along the line of the Canals and the Interior Commerce of the State of New York.* New York: T. and J. Swords, 1824.

Spoffords, Jeremiah. *Gazetteer of Massachusetts.* Newburyport, Mass.: C. Whipple, 1828.

"Stagecoach Stops, Coventry, Connecticut." *Colonial Homes,* vol. 17, no. 1, Feb. 1991.

Stommel, Henry and Stommel, Elizabeth. *Volcano Weather.* Newport, R.I.: Seven Seas Press, 1983.

Stuart, James. *Three Years in North America.* New York: J. & J. Harper, 1833.

Town of Burrillville Preliminary Survey Report. Providence: Rhode Island Historical Preservation and Heritage Commission, 1982.

Wallace, David H., ed. "From the Windows Of The Mail Coach." *The New-York Historical Society Quarterly,* vol. 1, no. 3, July 1956.

Watson, Elkanah. *History of the Rise, Progress, and existing Canals in the State of New York, etc.* Albany, 1820.

Watson, Winslow C. *Men and Times of the Revolution.* New York: D. Appleton & Co., 1861.

Wood, Frederick J. *The Turnpikes of New England.* Boston: Marshall Jones Co., 1919.

INDEX

Union College, 52
Unitarian, 92
United States Law Intelligence and Review, 4
Universalist Meeting House, 1
Utica, N.Y., x, xvi, 9, 10, 39, 52, 59, 64, 65
Uxbridge, Mass., 1

Varrick, Abraham, 27
Vincent, Chauncy, 61
Vincent, Elizabeth (Betsy) Joy, 13, 19
Vincent, Gardner, 72
Vincent, George R., 16
Vincent, Mrs. Nicholas, 54
Vincent, Nicholas, 13, 53, 65

Walden, John, 2
Wallace, Capt. James, 4
Ware, Mass., 3
Watson, Elkanah, 4, 52, 60, 75, 76
Watson, Emily, 4
Watson Tract, 24, 25; taxes, 47
Weather, 11, 17-19, 35, 38, 41, 43, 52, 55, 56, 58, 68, 70
Wells, Major (tavern keeper), 24
Welsh maid, 41
Welshmen, 67, 72
Western Hotel, 2
Western, Mass., 2
Wheeler, Capt., 72
White (hunter), 14, 15, 17, 4, 55, 58, 70
Williams (tavern keeper), 26
Williams, Roger, 1
Wister?, Eliza, 28, 59, 65
Wister, Dr. Owen, 28
Wool, 55
Worthington, Mass., 3, 63
Worthington Turnpike, 3